GDAŃSK
TRAVEL GUIDE
2024

Plan your visit today and uncover the treasures of this remarkable Polish gem

CAROLINE ZAHN

Title: GDAŃSK TRAVEL GUIDE 2024
Author: Caroline Zahn

Cover design by: [Caroline Zahn]
Interior design and formatting by: [Caroline Zahn]
For inquiries regarding permission , please contact the author at: [carolinezahn@gmail.com]
First edition : [JANUARY 2024]
ISBN: [N/A]

ABOUT THE AUTHOR

Caroline Zahn is a gifted writer who has a love of discovery and the capacity to lead other adventurers on the most amazing adventures. With the help of his extensive guidebook, Caroline Zahn turns routine travels into amazing experiences.

His work is evidence of his enduring wanderlust and his commitment to providing fellow travelers with priceless wisdom. As an experienced tourist, Caroline Zahn is aware of the subtleties involved in seeing new locations and engaging with other cultures. His guides are painstakingly written to provide cultural subtleties. His real love for discovering lesser-known aspects of places is evident in every page of his work, which equips readers with the necessary knowledge to set off on unforgettable journeys.

Caroline Zahn's work is distinguished by its captivating language and painstaking attention to detail. He has a natural capacity to take readers to distant places, allowing them to see themselves in the colorful villages, quiet countryside, and busy marketplaces he so eloquently describes. His enlightening travel advice transcends the apparent and gives readers a thorough grasp of the destinations they are going to see.

Caroline Zahn travel guides are a priceless asset, regardless of your level of experience and desire for new insights. Through his efforts, tourists are not only able to arrange a smooth trip but also thoroughly immerse themselves in the beauty and authenticity of their surroundings. With Caroline Zahn as your travel advisor, you can expect an adventure that will change and enrich you and leave a lasting impression on your heart and spirit.

TABLE OF CONTENTS

CHAPTER 1

INTRODUCTION

OVERVIEW OF GDAŃSK

Gdańsk, located along the magnificent Baltic Sea coastline, is a gem of northern Poland, attracting tourists with its rich history, architectural magnificence, and marine attractiveness. This fascinating city has played a critical role in determining the region's fate, evolving into a vibrant combination of old-world elegance and contemporary vigor. Discover Gdańsk's heart and soul by exploring its cobblestone streets and prominent sites.

Historical significance: Gdańsk has a rich history spanning millennia, seeing the rise and fall of several empires. The city's origins may be traced back to the tenth century when it was established as a thriving commercial center. Its advantageous position at the crossroads of key European trade routes helped to boost its economy by recruiting merchants and people from all across the continent.

During the Middle Ages, Gdańsk rose to prominence as a member of the Hanseatic League, marking a pivotal period in its history. The city's riches and importance during this time are reflected in its spectacular architecture, which includes the landmark Gothic-style St. Mary's Basilica and the towering Crane Gate, a testimony to its nautical heritage.

Gdańsk was a key player in the 20th-century battle for independence and human rights, known as the Solidarity Movement. In the 1980s, Lech Wałęsa's Solidarity movement centered around the historic Gdańsk Shipyard. This nonviolent revolution constituted a watershed moment in the battle against communist tyranny, ultimately leading to the crumbling of the Iron Curtain.

Gdańsk's skyline has a variety of architectural styles that reflect the city's numerous cultural influences. Wander around the Old Town, where painstakingly restored buildings take tourists back in time. The Gothic and Renaissance facades of merchant houses on Long Street (ulica Długa) and Long Market (Długi Targ) create an enchanting ambiance.

The Neptune Fountain, a reminder of the city's nautical past, stands above Long Market, while the Golden Gate greets tourists with exquisite decorations and allegorical statues. Gdańsk has the world's biggest brick church, St. Mary's Basilica. Visitors may climb to the top for panoramic views of the city.

Gdańsk's character is heavily influenced by its nautical background as a major port city. The Maritime Museum, located in the medieval Crane, offers an intriguing voyage through the city's naval past. Explore ships, navigational devices, and nautical relics to understand Gdańsk's history as a maritime superpower.

Gdańsk's rich history, architectural marvels, and maritime tradition provide a mesmerizing voyage through time. Gdańsk provides a variety of activities for both history aficionados and contemporary travelers, including wandering around the Old Town, learning about the city's revolutionary past, and admiring its architectural beauties. Come and experience the attraction of this Baltic jewel, where the past and present merge in a vivid celebration of culture and tradition.

BRIEF HISTORY

Gdańsk, a city with a rich history and magnificent architecture, exemplifies the perseverance and energy of its inhabitants. This quick historical review explores the important epochs that developed Gdańsk into the attractive city it is now.

Gdańsk's foundations date back to the 10th century, when a village called Gdania was formed. Gdańsk, located at the crossroads of key commercial routes along the Baltic Sea, rapidly became a lively trading city, drawing merchants from all over Europe. Its strategic position was critical to its early success, paving the way for centuries of marine and economic prominence.

During the Middle Ages, Gdańsk rose to prominence as a member of the Hanseatic League. This union of merchant guilds controlled commerce in the Baltic Sea and beyond. The city's prosperity was reflected in its spectacular Gothic architecture, which includes attractions like St. Mary's Basilica and the majestic Crane Gate. The elaborate façade of merchant homes along Long Street and Long Market were typical of Gdańsk's opulence during this golden age of commerce.

During the Royal and Prussian periods, the city's fortunes fluctuated based on historical events. Gdańsk had periods of royal administration under the Kingdom of Poland, but eventually fell under Prussian domination in the 18th century. The Prussian influence left an imprint on the city's architecture, merging with the older Gothic and Renaissance styles.

In the 20th century, Gdańsk became a symbol of resistance against repressive governments, representing solidarity and liberation. In the 1980s, Lech Wałęsa headed the Solidarity movement, which began in the Gdańsk Shipyard. This nonviolent revolution constituted a watershed moment in the battle against communism, eventually leading to the fall of the Iron Curtain and the victory of democracy in the area.

After the Cold War ended, Gdańsk had a post-Communist Renaissance. Embracing its history and cultural legacy, the city conducted massive restoration efforts, bringing new vitality to its old districts. The Old Town, with its cobblestone streets and colorful market squares, became a UNESCO World Heritage site, attracting people from all over the world.

Gdańsk's history is a remarkable tapestry of commerce, revolt, and persistence. From its modest origins as a trade outpost to its vital role in the war for independence, Gdańsk exemplifies the tenacious spirit of its people. Gdańsk's old streets and architectural wonders evoke echoes of years past, making it a living record of European history.

WHY VISIT GDAŃSK IN 2024

As 2024 approaches, tourists seeking an immersive and culturally stimulating experience are attracted to Gdańsk, where history comes to life and lively energy echoes through its picturesque alleyways. Here are convincing reasons why Gdańsk should be on top of your vacation itinerary in 2024.

Gdańsk is a living museum, displaying centuries of history via its well-preserved buildings and cobblestone streets. Explore the Old Town, a UNESCO World Heritage site, where Gothic and Renaissance monuments like St. Mary's Basilica and the Golden Gate transport you to another period. In 2024, continuing restoration operations will show the city's rich historical tapestry.

Visit the Gdańsk Shipyard, the cradle of the Solidarity movement, to experience its legacy. In 2024, this landmark will continue to be a symbol of the city's struggle for independence and human rights. Explore the European Solidarity Centre to learn about Gdańsk's impact on Eastern Europe's political environment.

Gdańsk has a variety of cultural festivals and events year-round. Check the calendar for events like the St. Dominic's Fair, one of the greatest commerce and cultural events in Europe, or the Gdańsk Shakespeare Festival, which celebrates the timeless works of the Bard in historic sites.

Gdańsk's seafaring heritage appeals to maritime lovers. To learn more about the city's nautical heritage, visit the Nautical Museum, which is situated in the renowned Crane. In 2024, new installations and interactive displays will illustrate Gdańsk's maritime superpower status.

Gdańsk has a thriving art scene with various galleries and street artworks. Immerse yourself in the local art culture, which includes both modern exhibits and traditional amber workmanship. Discover the Sołdek and Sea Towers, where art complements the city's coastal character.

Gdańsk's culinary culture combines traditional Polish cuisine with foreign influences. In 2024, enjoy local delights including pierogi, amber beer, and fresh Baltic fish at the quaint eateries that line the picturesque streets of the Old Town.

Gdańsk has accepted modernization while maintaining its ancient beauty. Excellent transit connections, including an international airport, make it readily accessible to visitors. Choose from a variety of lodgings, including boutique hotels in the Old Town and contemporary waterfront alternatives.

In 2024, Gdańsk offers a unique blend of history and modernity. Gdańsk offers a wonderful voyage across Europe, whether you're interested in its history, cultural events, or gastronomic adventures. Embrace the atmosphere of this Baltic treasure, where every pebble tells a tale and every moment invites exploration.

CHAPTER 2

PLANNING YOUR TRIP

BEST TIME TO VISIT

Gdańsk's rich history, maritime attractiveness, and dynamic cultural scene attract visitors throughout the year. However, choosing the best time to come may improve your experience, enabling you to take advantage of the city's numerous options. Discover the unique attractions of each season to choose the optimum time to experience Gdańsk's splendor.

1. Spring: Blooms and Renewal (April–June): Spring marks the end of winter in Gdańsk. The city's

parks and gardens come into flower, providing a magnificent setting for exploring. Spring provides a pleasant condition for strolling around the Old Town, dining at outdoor cafés, and attending cultural events, with temperatures ranging from 10 to 20 degrees Celsius (50-68°F). The St. Dominic's Fair in July symbolizes the end of spring and the start of Gdańsk's vibrant summer season.

2. Summer: Festival Vibes and Maritime Magic (July–August): Summer is the main season in Gdańsk, and with good reason. The city is bathed in pleasant sunshine, with average temperatures ranging from 18 to 25 degrees Celsius. The streets come alive with festivals, outdoor performances, and lively markets. The Baltic Sea provides a

cool respite, while Gdańsk's beaches attract sun lovers. While the crowds are higher, the vibrant mood and longer daylight hours make summer an ideal time to see the city's outdoor attractions.

3. Autumn: Amber Hues and Cultural Delights (September–November):
Autumn in Gdańsk gives a unique charm as temperatures drop. The city is drenched in warm colors, offering a magnificent environment for leisurely walks. With less people, you may visit museums, galleries, and historical places at a slower pace. The Gdańsk Shakespeare Festival, held in September, adds cultural value to your fall vacation.

4. Winter: Charming Festivities and Holiday Spirit (December–March): Winter turns Gdańsk into a magical realm. The Old Town is decorated with holiday lights, Christmas markets, and a lovely atmosphere. Although temperatures might drop below zero, Gdańsk's winter environment, along with fewer visitors, offers a unique and personal experience. Warm up with a cup of mulled wine and visit the city's pleasant interior attractions, including museums and historical places.

Choosing the ideal time to visit Gdańsk relies on your tastes and desired experiences. Gdańsk offers a variety of experiences throughout the year, including the flowering beauty of spring, the bustling festivals of summer, the quiet charm of autumn, and the spectacular winter celebrations.

VISA REQUIREMENTS

Planning a vacation to Gdańsk requires not only soaking in its rich history and lively culture but also securing proper travel paperwork. Understanding the visa requirements is an important step in planning for your visit to this Polish treasure.

Gdańsk, like the rest of Poland, is part of the Schengen Area. This provides for smooth travel among 27 European nations without internal border inspections. Visitors from countries that are also members of the Schengen Agreement normally do not need a visa for short visits of up to 90 days within 180 days.

Visa-Free Travel: EU citizens, as well as those from the US, Canada, Australia, and Japan, may visit Poland and Gdańsk without a visa for short visits. However, it is essential to evaluate the particular entrance criteria and length of stay permitted under the visa-free system.

To visit Gdańsk, citizens of non-visa-exempt countries must apply for a Schengen visa. This visa is normally provided for short-term trips and permits travel inside the Schengen Zone. Application methods and criteria may differ, therefore it is best to contact the Polish embassy or consulate in your home country for the most current and up-to-date information.

Extended stays, including job or study, may need a separate visa category. Long-stay national visas are necessary for stays of more than 90 days and must be secured before coming to Poland. The specific criteria and paperwork differ depending on the objective of your travel, such as job, study, or other long-term obligations.

To obtain a Schengen visa or a long-stay national visa, you must provide a completed application form, a valid passport, proof of travel arrangements, travel insurance, proof of accommodation, and any supporting documents related to your visit. It is critical to begin the application procedure well in advance of your intended trip date to account for any processing delays.

To plan a trip to Gdańsk, it's important to understand the visa requirements. Whether you're touring the ancient alleys of the Old Town or staying for a long period, ensuring your travel documents meet Polish rules will help you have a seamless and comfortable journey in this charming city by the Baltic Sea. Always check with the appropriate authorities for the most up-to-date visa information and requirements before making travel plans.

CURRENCY AND BUDGETING TIPS

To fully enjoy your trip to Gdańsk, it's important to learn about the local currency and budget wisely. Learn about monetary basics and budgeting suggestions for a pleasant vacation in Gdańsk, from seeing historic monuments to enjoying local food.

The Polish złoty (PLN) is the official currency in Gdańsk and across Poland. While bigger institutions and tourist attractions may take credit cards, it is best to have cash on hand for smaller shops, local markets, and transportation. ATMs are extensively accessible in Gdańsk, making it easier to withdraw złoty when required.

Before your travel, check current exchange rates to make educated currency exchange selections. While converting money at the airport or in the city is usual, be wary of hidden costs and less favorable rates. Consider withdrawing cash from ATMs for reasonable rates and the convenience of using local currency.

Major credit cards like Visa and MasterCard are frequently accepted in Gdańsk, particularly at hotels, restaurants, and bigger retailers. However, you should notify your bank of your trip dates to prevent any possible card transaction complications. Smaller businesses and marketplaces may prefer cash, therefore having a mix of both methods of payment is advisable.

Budgeting for Accommodation: Gdańsk provides a variety of accommodations, including boutique hotels in the Old Town and contemporary waterfront lodgings. Prices vary depending on location, facilities, and time of year. Consider reserving ahead of time to ensure low prices, and look at a variety of hotel options to discover the best fit for your needs and budget.

Gdańsk, like the rest of Poland, is known for its economical and wonderful food. Dining at local eateries and street food booths delivers a genuine experience at a reasonable cost. Set aside a chunk of your cash to sample classic foods like pierogi and złoty-perogies. Explore the varied gastronomic offers dispersed across the city.

Gdańsk has a well-connected public transit infrastructure, including buses and trams, allowing for easy exploration of the city and environs. Budget for transportation expenses depending on your intended activities, and consider getting multi-day tickets for further savings. Taxis are also available; however, rates should be confirmed in advance or used with trustworthy ride-sharing services.

Entrance fees apply to several historic sites and museums in Gdańsk. Plan your plan and budget for entrance to attractions like St. Mary's Basilica, the Maritime Museum, and the European

Solidarity Centre. Some attractions offer cheap or free admission on specified days, so check timetables and plan accordingly.

Gdańsk offers a variety of experiences for tourists, and careful budgeting allows them to fully appreciate the city's attractions. This advice will help you make the most of your time in Gdańsk, enabling you to concentrate on making memorable experiences. They include recognizing currency intricacies and budgeting for different costs.

TRANSPORTATION OPTIONS

Gdańsk's dynamic atmosphere and rich history make it a place worth exploring. Understanding the many transportation choices available is critical for making the most of your vacation. Here's a thorough guide to traversing Gdańsk, including fast public transit and convenient taxi options.

Gdańsk's well-organized public transit infrastructure allows tourists to easily explore the city and neighboring regions. The network consists of buses and trams operated by ZTM. Tickets may be bought at ticket machines, kiosks, or from the driver. Consider getting a day or multi-day ticket to allow unrestricted movement throughout the city.

Gdańsk is a bicycle-friendly city, with dedicated lanes and rental services. Exploring the city on two wheels offers a distinct viewpoint, letting you cover more territory and find hidden jewels. Bike rental firms often charge hourly or daily rates, making it an environmentally responsible and cost-effective mode of transportation.

Taxis are a handy means of transportation in Gdańsk, particularly for people who want to reach their location without stopping. Ensure that you use regulated taxi services, and confirm the fare with the driver before beginning the trip. Ride-sharing services are also available and provide a dependable option.

Gdańsk's position along the Baltic Sea makes boat transit an ideal method to see the city. Water trams on the Motława River provide picturesque views of the riverfront and Old Town. Boat trips provide a relaxing opportunity to discover Gdańsk from a unique viewpoint.

Car Rentals: While Gdańsk's public transit system makes it simple to traverse the city without a car, travelers seeking to visit the neighboring areas may consider renting one. Gdańsk has many international and local rental firms that provide flexibility and convenience for day excursions or longer vacations.

Walking is a great way to experience the charm of Gdańsk. The Old Town, with its cobblestone streets and medieval buildings, is pedestrian-friendly, enabling you to take your time exploring its small lanes and squares. Many of the city's attractions, such as St. Mary's Basilica and the Neptune Fountain, are easily accessible on foot.

Airport Transportation: Gdańsk Lech Wałęsa Airport offers convenient access to the city. The airport is connected to different regions of Gdańsk by public buses, airport shuttles, and taxis. Furthermore, several hotels provide airport transfers for extra convenience.

Gdańsk has a variety of transportation choices to help tourists explore the city comfortably and effectively. Gdańsk's transportation network offers a variety of options, including public transit, bicycle and vehicle rentals, and stunning views from the water tram.

CHAPTER 3

GETTING ACQUAINTED WITH GDAŃSK

CITY LAYOUT AND NEIGHBORHOODS

Gdańsk, a city rich in history and architectural wonders, has a distinct layout and different districts. Navigating the city becomes a trip through time as you discover the distinct features of each neighborhood. Explore Gdańsk's many neighborhoods and city layout.

Gdańsk's Old Town, known as Stare Miasto, reflects the city's medieval and Hanseatic origins. The Old

Town, known for its narrow cobblestone alleys, Gothic and Renaissance architecture, and lively market squares, is home to prominent sites like the Neptune Fountain, the Main Town Hall, and the Arthur's Court. Long Street (Ulica Długa) and Long Market (Długi Targ) are the bustling spines of the Old Town, with colorful facades and busy cafés.

The Main City (Główne Miasto) lies next to the Old Town and has meandering alleys and scenic squares that add to its historical appeal. This neighborhood has a combination of historic buildings, bustling cultural events, and a variety of food alternatives. The Main City is home to the renowned Mariacka Street, noted for its amber stores, as well as the spectacular St. Mary's Basilica, the world's biggest brick church.

Główne Miasto Przedmieście, located north of the Main City, is a residential area with a peaceful environment. Local markets, parks, and a more laid-back lifestyle may all be found here. This area offers an insight into daily life in Gdańsk and is a welcome respite from the busy city center.

Śródmieście, or "city center," is a vibrant district that blends historical elegance with contemporary facilities. This neighborhood is famous for its commercial lanes, numerous eateries, and modern architecture. Śródmieście's location near the Main Railway Station and key transportation hubs makes it an ideal starting point for exploring Gdańsk.

Oliwa, located north of the city center, offers a unique combination of natural beauty and cultural depth. The Oliwa Cathedral, which is encircled by a garden and famous for its Baroque organ recitals, is a highlight. Oliwa Park, with its strolling trails and ponds, provides a calm respite, making it an ideal neighborhood for people looking for a more peaceful environment.

Przymorze and Brzeźno, located northwest of Gdańsk, are seaside neighborhoods that provide a unique perspective on the city. Brzeźno Beach is a popular attraction with a sandy beach and vibrant promenade. Przymorze's modern architecture and recreational spaces provide a contemporary contrast to the city's historic heart.

Wrzeszcz, located west of the city center, is a busy quarter with quirky businesses and a diverse range of architectural types. The Gdańsk University campus in Wrzeszcz contributes to the young and vibrant ambiance. The neighborhood is well accessible by public transit, making it simple to explore.

Gdańsk's city structure and districts are a fascinating blend of history, culture, and modernity. Each area has its distinct personality, adding to the rich tapestry of this Baltic treasure. Gdańsk offers a diverse range of experiences, from the ancient Old Town to the modern Wrzeszcz.

LOCAL CULTURE AND CUSTOMS

Gdańsk, known for its nautical heritage and strong attitude, also has a lively local culture created by centuries of influence. Understanding local customs and traditions enhances the authenticity of your Gdańsk experience, as you tour its picturesque streets and interact with its kind locals.

Gdańsk is known for its amber handicraft, which is profoundly rooted in local culture. Amber jewelry, with complex motifs, is a favorite keepsake. Visitors may visit several amber stores, notably those on Mariacka Street, where experienced artists display their wares. It is typical to browse and interact with the craftspeople to learn more about this valuable Baltic jewel.

Gdańsk's history as a port city makes marine heritage an important part of local culture. The renowned Gdańsk Crane, originally used for loading and unloading ships, represents the city's naval past. Explore Gdańsk's maritime history at the Maritime Museum. Don't miss the chance to meet residents who are enthusiastic about their nautical traditions on the waterfront.

Gdańsk's cultural narrative is heavily influenced by the Solidarity movement, which originated in the city's shipyard in the 1980s. The European Solidarity Centre stands as a symbol of the battle for workers' rights and freedom. Engage with locals to learn more about this critical period in Polish history, and pay tribute to those who struggled for justice and democracy at sites such as the Monument of the Fallen Shipyard Workers.

Gdańsk's local culture values Polish food, which is known for its substantial and savory meals. Enjoy traditional dishes like pierogi (dumplings), żurek (sour rye soup), and bigos (hunter's stew). Local markets, such as Hala Targowa, provide a genuine experience, enabling you to try regional delicacies and interact with merchants who are enthusiastic about their culinary history.

Gdańsk has several cultural festivals and events throughout the year. The St. Dominic's Fair, one of the greatest commerce and cultural festivals in Europe, celebrates Gdańsk's mercantile legacy. The Gdańsk Shakespeare Festival, conducted yearly, highlights the city's cultural variety via the arts. Participating in these events gives you a direct glimpse of the city's vibrant and social character.

Respect for Tradition: Polish culture values tradition and legacy. When entering houses or holy locations, it is traditional to remove your shoes as a show of respect. Gdańsk's ancient churches, such as St. Mary's Basilica, provide a glimpse into religious practices and traditions. Visitors are urged to examine these buildings with respect.

Locals in Gdańsk are noted for their kind nature and great welcome. Engage with locals at cafés, markets, or cultural events, and you can find yourself in deep discussions about the city's history, customs, and everyday life. A polite "Dzień dobry" (Good day) and genuine curiosity in the local culture might lead to important interactions.

Immersing oneself in Gdańsk's local culture offers a glimpse into a society influenced by history, perseverance, and real friendliness. Whether enjoying amber artistry, relishing traditional meals, or participating in cultural activities, embracing the local traditions strengthens your connection to this Baltic treasure and assures a genuine and rewarding experience in the heart of Poland.

LANGUAGE ESSENTIALS

Understanding the local language might enhance your experience in Gdańsk, connecting you to the city's dynamic culture. While English is widely spoken in tourist destinations, learning a few Polish words may improve your experience and lead to meaningful contact with people.

The official language of Gdańsk, like the rest of Poland, is Polish. Polish is a Slavic language with a distinctive alphabet and accent. Many Poles, particularly in metropolitan places like Gdańsk, speak English. However, showing interest in their original language is generally welcomed and may develop a favorable connection.

Learning the fundamental language will help you navigate everyday encounters more effectively. Here are some key phrases in Polish:

- Hello: A good day (Jen DOH-bri)
- Goodbye: Regarding viewing (Doh Veet-ZEHN-ya)
- Please: Proszę (proh-sheh).
- Thank you! Dziękuję (djen-KOO-yeh)
- Yes: Tak (tahk).
- No: Nie (Nyeh)

- Excuse me/I apologize: Przepraszam (pshe-PRAH-sham)
- Good Morning: Good day (DOH-bri)
- Good evening! Excellent work. (DOH-bri, YEH-chor)
- My name is: Nazywam się (nah-ZIV-am sheh).

Polish pronunciation: Polish pronunciation might be difficult for non-native speakers owing to the distinct sounds of some letters. Listening to native speakers and using language applications or internet resources might help you improve your pronunciation. Pay attention to consonants such as ś, cz, ż, and ł, which have unique sounds.

Language Apps and Resources: Apps like Duolingo, Babbel, and Rosetta Stone provide Polish courses for further learning. Online platforms and language exchange programs may link you with native speakers to practice. Local libraries and language schools in Gdańsk may provide immersive learning opportunities.

English is frequently spoken in Gdańsk, particularly in tourist-friendly places like hotels and restaurants. Many younger Poles speak English well, and locals working in tourism are likely to converse successfully in English. However, demonstrating an attempt to speak Polish is often greeted with excitement and praise.

To use public transit, it's important to know popular terminology, even if the signage includes English translations.

- Autobus (ow-TO-boss).
- Tram: tramwaj (TRAHM-vai)
- Ticket: Bilet (pronounced bee-let).
- Train Station: Dworzec Kolejowy (DVOCH-zest kolei-OH-vi).
- Metro (pronounced MEH-tro)

Cultural Sensitivity: When communicating, it is important to consider cultural differences. Politeness and formality are very important in Polish culture. Addressing people with the appropriate titles, using "Pan" for

Mr. and "Pani" for Mrs./Ms., demonstrates respect.

Embracing the language essentials of Gdańsk is not only a practical way to navigate the city but also a respectful gesture towards its culture and people.
While English will serve you well, the effort to speak a bit of Polish can lead to more enriching experiences, fostering connections and creating lasting memories in this captivating Baltic city.

CHAPTER 4

TOP ATTRACTIONS

THE ROYAL WAY

Gdańsk, a city rich in history and architectural magnificence, welcomes you to explore the Royal Way (Droga Królewska). This renowned path connects historic sites while meandering through the center of the Old Town, allowing you to follow in the footsteps of monarchs, statesmen, and merchants who once traversed these fabled streets. Join us in exploring Gdańsk's lovely Royal Way.

The Royal Way starts at the Upland Gate (Brama Wyżynna), the western entrance to the Old Town. From here, the path meanders through the Long Street (Ulica Długa) and the Long Market (Długi Targ), covering roughly 1,000 meters of gorgeous cobblestone streets flanked with perfectly maintained ancient houses.

The Upland Gate (Brama Wyżynna) was built in the 16th century and serves as a spectacular entrance to the Royal Way. The entrance to Gdańsk's Old Town, adorned with Renaissance ornamentation and crested with the city's coat of arms, transports visitors to a bygone age.

Long Street (Ulica Długa) has well-preserved merchant buildings, each with a distinct tale about Gdańsk's affluent history. Admire the Neptune Fountain, a reminder of the city's nautical supremacy, and the magnificent Artus Court (Dwór Artusa), which was formerly a gathering place for merchants and officials.

The Royal Way leads to the Long Market, a busy area with colorful townhouses and the Green Gate (Brama Zielona) at one end. During Polish monarchs' travels to Gdańsk, they used to stay at the Green Gate, which has Flemish elements.

The Golden Gate (Brama Złota) is a triumphal arch capped with a sculpture of King John III Sobieski on horseback. This gate functioned as a ceremonial entry to the city, setting the tone for the grandeur of the Royal Way.

The Main Town Hall (Ratusz Głównego Miasta) dominates the skyline of the Royal Way and represents Gdańsk's medieval wealth. Its clock tower gives a panoramic perspective of the city. Explore the interiors to learn about the rich history and amazing architecture of this renowned monument.

The Royal Way culminates with St. Mary's Basilica, the world's biggest brick church. Admire the Gothic architecture, climb the tower for stunning views, and take in the delicate features of the astronomical clock. The Basilica provides a perfect climax to the Royal Way, leaving tourists in awe.

Explore the Amber Court (Dwór Artusa) near St. Mary's Basilica to end your regal adventure. This ancient building's amber-themed exhibitions honor Gdańsk's famous legacy of amber manufacture.

The Royal Way of Gdańsk is more than just a path; it's a voyage through history and a glimpse into a bygone period. As you walk down this royal road, the architectural marvels, historic monuments, and tangible feeling of legacy will transport you to a time when monarchs and merchants once influenced the fate of this Baltic treasure. The Royal Way tells the story of Gdańsk's history with each step, letting visitors participate in the eternal drama.

OLD TOWN HIGHLIGHTS

Gdańsk's Old Town offers a fascinating blend of history, architecture, and culture, allowing visitors to experience the city's rich legacy. With cobblestone alleys, historic houses, and lovely squares, the Old Town tells a riveting story. Discover why Gdańsk's Old Town is a must-see for both history buffs and travelers.

The Upland Gate (Brama Wyżynna) is a magnificent entrance point to Gdańsk's Old Town, embellished with Renaissance decoration. This gate, built in the 16th century, acted as both a defense barrier and the city's ceremonial entry. The elaborate features and intimidating grandeur set the tone for the ancient treasures that await beyond.

Long Street (Ulica Długa) has well-preserved townhouses that are a sight to see. The facades reflect a variety of architectural styles, including Gothic, Renaissance, and Baroque. Admire the beautiful Neptune Fountain and the bustling Artus Court, which previously held merchants and officials. Long Street is a walkway that takes visitors through Gdańsk's commercial history.

Long Market (Długi Targ) is a busy area surrounded by elegant townhouses, effortlessly transitioning from Royal Way. The Neptune Fountain, a symbol of Gdańsk's maritime history, is prominently displayed in the center. The Green Gate at the end of the market housed visiting Polish rulers. The cobblestone area is packed with bright cafés, providing an ideal site to take in the vibe.

Gdańsk's Golden Gate (Brama Złota) is a triumphal arch that reflects the city's magnificence. This gate, adorned with sculptures and reliefs, served as the city's ceremonial entry. The architectural beauty of Gdańsk conveys the city's rich past.

The Main Town Hall (Ratusz Głównego Miasta) is a prominent landmark in Gdańsk's Old Town, featuring an impressive clock tower. This Gothic masterpiece functioned as the center of municipal authority and trade.

Climb the tower for panoramic views of the city, and tour the interiors to see council chambers and historical objects that depict the story of Gdańsk's government.

St. Mary's Basilica (Bazylika Mariacka), the world's biggest brick church, is a highlight of Gdańsk's Old Town. The stunning Gothic architecture and elaborate features make it a must-see. Ascend the tower for panoramic views of the city, and see the cosmic splendor of the astronomical clock within.

Mariacka Street, with its cobblestone beauty and unusual architecture, is known for its amber commerce. Explore the tiny stores that sell excellent amber jewelry, and take in the atmosphere of this old street. Mariacka Street is a hidden treasure in Gdańsk's Old Town, offering a lovely combination of history and workmanship.

The Amber Court (Dwór Artusa), located near St. Mary's Basilica, is a historic edifice that honors Gdańsk's famous amber workmanship. Engage with the exhibitions that highlight the importance of amber in the city's history, and bask in the golden glow of this valuable Baltic treasure.

Gdańsk's Old Town exemplifies the city's durability, wealth, and cultural vitality across centuries. Each step through Upland Gate, Long Street, and beyond reveals architectural marvels, cultural riches, and the resilient soul of this Baltic gem. Experience the charm of Gdańsk's Old Town, where every nook tells a tale and every square vibrates with history.

SOLIDARITY SQUARE AND MONUMENT

Gdańsk is known for its maritime heritage and architectural magnificence, but it also has heartbreaking sites that commemorate the battle for workers' rights and independence. Solidarity Square, with its famous Monument to the Fallen Shipyard Workers, is a vivid reminder of the tenacious spirit of the Solidarity movement, which shaped contemporary Polish history. Learn about the importance and meaning of Solidarity Square and the Monument in Gdańsk.

Solidarity Square, formerly Victory Square, rose to worldwide prominence throughout the turbulent 20th century. The Solidarity movement, founded by Lech Wałęsa, originated in the Gdańsk Shipyard in 1980. The movement, which sprang from labor strikes and demands for workers' rights, became a catalyst for change, ultimately contributing to the demise of communism in Poland.

Solidarity Square has the Monument to the Fallen Shipyard Workers (Pomnik Poległych Stoczniowców), a powerful emblem of resistance and solidarity.

Unveiled in 1980, the monument was built by artist Władysław Hasior and remembers the workers who died during the December 1970 demonstrations.

Architectural Symbolism: The memorial design reflects the Solidarity movement's ambitions and sacrifices. The towering three crosses, dramatically silhouetted against the sky, embody the principles of freedom, unity, and solidarity. The shipyard gate commemorates the Gdańsk Shipyard's key role in the formation of the Solidarity movement.

A plaque beside the monument commemorates the shipyard workers who died during the December 1970 demonstrations.

Inscriptions in Polish and other languages honor the workers' tenacity and the victory of the Solidarity movement, recognizing its influence on the path of European history.

The Solidarity Centre (Europejskie Centrum Solidarności) is located near Solidarity Square and has a contemporary architecture that blends well with its historic surroundings. The facility functions as a museum, exhibition space, and educational hub committed to preserving the memory of the Solidarity movement. Visitors may explore multimedia exhibitions, relics, and papers that detail the events leading up to the movement's founding.

Solidarity Square is a dynamic area for commemorating, uniting, and celebrating the spirit of solidarity. This iconic square is often used to commemorate important events, as well as host international conferences and debates.

Solidarity Square is widely accessible in Gdańsk, and tourists are urged to explore and appreciate its historical importance. Guided tours of the square and the Solidarity Centre provide in-depth insights into the historical backdrop and lasting influence of the Solidarity movement.

Unity Square and the Monument to the Fallen Shipyard Workers are strong symbols of resistance, freedom, and unity. Standing in front of these historic sites in

Gdańsk transports you to a period when the collective voice of workers rang through the shipyard, sparking a movement that shaped Poland's future and inspired liberation movements worldwide. It is a location where history lives on, and echoes of the past continue to inspire current and future generations.

GDAŃSK SHIPYARDS

Gdańsk, a city rich in nautical heritage, owes much of its worldwide prominence to the famed Gdańsk Shipyards. Gdańsk's shipyards, known for shipbuilding and the cradle of the Solidarity movement, demonstrate the city's resilience, ingenuity, and historical significance. Let's study the interesting narrative of the Gdańsk Shipyards.

Historical Background: The Gdańsk Shipyards have a long history extending back to the Middle Ages. Established in 1945, the shipyards played an important part in Poland's postwar rehabilitation and became a cornerstone of the country's marine sector. The shipyards gained worldwide recognition for their skill and inventiveness, bolstering the city's image as a marine powerhouse.

In 1980, the Gdańsk Shipyards became the focal point of the Solidarity movement, marking a watershed event in contemporary European history. Led by electrician Lech Wałęsa, shipyard workers went on strike to demand workers' rights and political changes. The Gdańsk Agreement, signed in the shipyards, established the autonomous labor union Solidarity, challenging the Communist authority and triggering events that eventually led to the collapse of communism in Poland.

The European Solidarity Centre (Europejskie Centrum Solidarności), located near the Gdańsk Shipyards, commemorates the events of 1980. This cultural institution functions as a museum, teaching center, and archive, all devoted to preserving the legacy of the Solidarity movement. Visitors may explore multimedia exhibitions, relics, and immersive displays to get a thorough grasp of this transformational age.

The Monument to the Fallen Shipyard Workers may be seen at Solidarity Square, located inside the shipyard complex. The monument, unveiled in 1980, serves as a mournful homage to the shipyard workers who died during the December 1970 demonstrations, as well as a strong symbol of the Solidarity movement's principles.

Gdańsk Shipyard Today:
While the shipyards have changed in recent decades to adapt to economic developments and market needs, they are still active and contribute to Poland's marine sector. The shipyard complex has expanded its operations to include ship repairs, steel production, and manufacturing.

The shipyard complex has historical monuments, including the Gdańsk Crane, a medieval structure used for freight loading and unloading. The relics of the shipyard's industrial legacy are visible, resulting in a distinct combination of the old and modern.

Guided tours are provided to learn about the Gdańsk Shipyards' history, shipbuilding process, and the effect of the Solidarity movement. Knowledgeable interpreters provide tales that bring the shipyards' history to life, making for a fascinating and educational experience for visitors.

The Gdańsk Shipyards, with its maritime tradition and historical significance, are still an important element of the city's character.

Gdańsk's shipyards embody perseverance, solidarity, and reinvention, having played a major part in the Solidarity movement and establishing the city on the world map. Exploring the Gdańsk Shipyards is more than simply a voyage through maritime history; it's an immersion into the stories that have defined Gdańsk's fate and left an indelible stamp on the path of European history.

OLIWA CATHEDRAL AND PARK

The Oliwa Cathedral and its surrounding park, located in northern Gdańsk, provide a peaceful getaway from the city's hustle and bustle. This ensemble, steeped in history, embellished with Baroque brilliance, and surrounded by the green Oliwa Park, forms a peaceful refuge where visitors may immerse themselves in architectural beauty, spiritual reflection, and natural quiet.

Oliwa Cathedral (Archikatedra Oliwska), also known as the Archcathedral Basilica of the Holy Trinity, Blessed Virgin Mary, and St. Bernard, is a masterpiece of Baroque architecture. The cathedral, which dates back to the 13th century, underwent substantial modifications in the 18th century to become the sumptuous masterpiece that it is today. The facade, embellished with exquisite sculptures and rich details, alludes to the grandeur within.

Experience the splendor of Baroque art at Oliwa Cathedral. Admire the wonderfully built altars, gorgeous pulpit, and amazing pipe organ. The cathedral's main attraction is the famed Oliwa Organ, a masterwork of organ architecture with rich tones and beautiful carvings. Regular organ performances are given, enabling visitors to enjoy the cathedral's acoustic magnificence.

Oliwa Park (Park Oliwski) surrounds the cathedral and offers groomed lawns, meandering walks, and scenic ponds. Established in the 18th century, the park blends in with the cathedral's aura, providing a perfect setting where history, architecture, and nature meet.

Oliwa Park has ancient structures and sculptures that enhance its appeal. The Witches' Well, a unique octagonal well with a fascinating mythology, serves as a focal point. The park also has statues of legendary characters, which provide an artistic touch to the natural scenery.

The Abbot's Palace (Pałac Opatów), located in Oliwa Park, exudes royal magnificence. Originally a retreat for Cistercian abbots, the palace's Baroque design and planted gardens make it an enjoyable stop for visitors to the park.

The Oliwa Botanical Garden, located next to Oliwa Park, is a botanical paradise with a rich array of plant species. The garden offers a peaceful setting for leisurely walks, surrounded by rare and exotic species. The Oliwa Botanical Garden is a hidden gem among the larger Oliwa Cathedral and Park complex.

Oliwa Cathedral is significant for religious reasons, since it houses the Archbishop of Gdańsk. The cathedral's spiritual aura, along with its calm surroundings, gives it a haven for introspection and contemplation.

When visiting Oliwa Cathedral and Park, be sure to check the calendar for upcoming organ performances. Exploring the park is best done on a leisurely stroll, which allows you to appreciate the historic monuments and natural splendor.

Oliwa Cathedral and Park provide a diverse experience, including Baroque art, spiritual reflection, and natural walks. The harmonized combination captures Gdańsk's cultural and natural resources, creating a refuge where the past and present combine in a timeless celebration of beauty and peace.

CHAPTER 5

MUSEUMS AND GALLERIES

NATIONAL MARITIME MUSEUM

The National Maritime Museum in Gdańsk, a city known for its maritime heritage, offers an interactive experience that takes visitors through centuries of naval history, exploration, and invention. Located in old buildings along the waterfront, the museum is a nautical treasure trove that provides a thorough look at Poland's naval history. Explore the National Marine Museum in

Gdańsk and discover its marine treasures.

The National Maritime Museum, located on the scenic Motława River, is housed in ancient structures such as Granaries Island (Wyspa Spichrzów) and the Crane (Żuraw). The architecture of Gdańsk reflects the city's nautical tradition, with red-brick warehouses and buildings dating back centuries.

The National Maritime Museum has the renowned Crane (Żuraw), which dominates the riverside skyline. This medieval crane, which was originally used to load and unload goods from ships, is one of the best-preserved medieval port cranes in Europe. Visitors may climb the Crane for a panoramic view of the city and river.

The National Marine Museum has numerous display halls featuring a variety of marine relics, models, and historical exhibitions. Permanent and temporary exhibits focus on topics such as navigation, shipbuilding, marine commerce, and the Polish Navy's storied past.

The Marine Culture Center (Centrum Kultury Morskiej) at the museum aims to promote marine traditions and preserve cultural assets. Visitors may take part in workshops, activities, and educational programs that explore marine cultures, crafts, and the distinctive way of life linked with the sea.

The Ship Mill (Stara Stocznia-Młyn): The Ship-Mill, a rebuilt medieval vessel that historically played an important role in grain milling and port activities, is a standout feature of the museum. The Ship-Mill offers a hands-on experience, enabling visitors to appreciate the clever engineering of these old marine equipment.

The National Maritime Museum oversees various historical shipyard sites, including the open-air exhibitions on Shipyard Island and the Sołdek Museum Ship. These locations provide a genuine view of shipbuilding processes, showing boats and marine infrastructure that played important roles in Gdańsk's maritime history.

The museum promotes marine education via various programs, seminars, and workshops for visitors of all ages. These programs seek to instill a love of nautical history, navigation, and the sciences linked with sailing.

The National Maritime Museum organizes events and festivals throughout the year. The museum's festivals include sea shanties, historical reenactments, and festivities honoring Gdańsk's nautical heritage.

Before visiting a museum, check the calendar for any temporary exhibits, special events, or guided tours. The museum's position on the Motława River makes it conveniently accessible. Combining a visit with a walk along the riverfront enriches the whole experience.

The National Nautical Museum in Gdańsk is more than simply a collection of relics. It takes visitors on a journey through time, revealing the stories of mariners, explorers, and shipbuilders who established Poland's nautical identity. From the towering Crane to the hands-on activities in the ship mill, every element of the museum echoes nautical history. The National Maritime Museum offers a fascinating insight into Gdańsk's maritime history.

ST. MARY'S CHURCH MUSEUM

St. Mary's Church dominates the skyline of Gdańsk's Old Town, reflecting the city's rich history and spiritual legacy. The St. Mary's Church Museum is located inside the sacred walls of this great Gothic cathedral, and it houses religious items, art treasures, and a centuries-long story of faith. Join us on a tour to discover the holy and artistic delights of the historic St. Mary's Church Museum.

St. Mary's Church, or Basilica of the Assumption of the Blessed Virgin Mary, is the world's biggest brick church. Its construction began in the 14th century and took over 150 years to finish. The church's towering towers and elaborate façade embody the majesty of Gothic architecture, providing an impressive presence in Gdańsk's skyline.

St. Mary's Church is historically notable for more than only its architecture. Gdańsk residents used it for religion, faith, and civic pride. The church was crucial throughout numerous times, including the Reformation and the city's quest for independence.

The St. Mary's Church Museum, located inside the basilica, showcases religious art, cultural heritage, and the history of religion in Gdańsk. The museum offers a glimpse into the spiritual and creative journeys of the church and its members.

The museum has a vast collection of religious items, altarpieces, and holy utensils dating back centuries. Admire finely carved wooden altars, illuminated manuscripts, and liturgical garments that demonstrate the skill and commitment of past artists and worshipers.

The astronomical clock at St. Mary's Church is a 15th-century masterpiece of workmanship. Visitors may marvel at the complex moving pieces and symbolic representations of cosmic occurrences, seeing the intersection of art and science in medieval timekeeping.

Explore the museum to see the chapels and side altars of the cathedral. Each chapel offers a distinct tale via religious art, statuary, and memorial inscriptions. The Chapel of the Holy Virgin Mary is well-known for its magnificent beauty and historical importance.

St. Mary's Church honors slain seamen via maritime-themed chapels and monuments. Gdańsk has always been a coastal city, thus these monuments represent the symbiotic link between the water and the faithful who rely on it for their livelihood.

When visiting St. Mary's Church Museum, take a guided tour to learn more about the basilica's history and artwork. Check the church's calendar for any special events, religious services, or performances that may complement your visit.

St. Mary's Church Museum in Gdańsk combines spirituality with art, providing a holy and culturally rich experience for visitors. St. Mary's Church, with its towering spires, antique treasures, and powerful echoes of centuries of devotion, stands not only as a witness to faith, but also as a living museum that preserves Gdańsk's religious and artistic legacy.

EUROPEAN SOLIDARITY CENTRE

The European Solidarity Centre (Europejskie Centrum Solidarności) on Gdańsk's historic waterfront honors the spirit of solidarity, which played a significant role in defining contemporary European history. This vibrant cultural institution is a living witness to the Solidarity movement and its revolutionary influence on the fight for workers' rights and, ultimately, the fall of communism. Join us on a tour around the European Solidarity Centre to explore stories of perseverance, freedom, and the quest of human dignity.

The European Solidarity Centre's modern architecture integrates well with the neighboring older buildings. The architecture of the building represents the ideas of the Solidarity movement, which emphasizes openness and transparency. Its stunning shape and unique characteristics make it a contemporary icon that also pays tribute to the historical events it remembers.

The Centre aims to preserve the memory of the Solidarity movement, which began in the Gdańsk Shipyard in 1980. Led by Lech Wałęsa, the movement brought together workers seeking improved working conditions, human rights, and political change. The Gdańsk Agreement, signed in the shipyards, established the independent labor union Solidarity and sparked a countrywide movement to oppose the Communist authority.

The European Solidarity Centre's permanent displays highlight the major events of the Solidarity movement. Engaging multimedia exhibits, historical relics, and interactive installations take visitors through the history of strikes, demonstrations, and the final victory of Solidarity's values. The story goes beyond Poland, demonstrating the movement's impact across Europe.

The Centre's main exhibition, Roads to Freedom, takes visitors through the turbulent years of the Solidarity movement. Divided into themed parts, this immersive display delves into the important events, people, and larger societal background that inspired the movement, offering a thorough grasp of its historical importance.

The Centre's Voices of Solidarity exhibit features first-hand tales and testimonies from active participants in the movement, making it a powerful experience for visitors. The voices of workers, intellectuals, and ordinary people portray the personal sacrifices, victories, and communal spirit that marked Solidarity.

The European Solidarity Centre periodically presents temporary exhibits, cultural events, and educational activities to supplement its permanent displays. These initiatives delve into contemporary issues, human rights, and the ongoing struggle for solidarity in various contexts worldwide.

The Centre promotes knowledge and understanding via educational programs, seminars, and lectures. These initiatives cater to students, scholars, and the general public, encouraging dialogue and critical reflection on the principles of solidarity, democracy, and civic engagement.

Libraries and Archives: The Centre houses extensive libraries and archives containing a wealth of documents, photographs, and publications related to the Solidarity movement. Scholars and researchers have access to these resources, contributing to the academic study of this pivotal period in European history.

Memorial Sites: Adjacent to the Centre, visitors can explore the Monument to the Fallen Shipyard Workers, a powerful tribute to those who lost their lives during the December 1970 protests.

The monument serves as a solemn reminder of the sacrifices made in the pursuit of freedom and social justice.

Visiting Tips: When planning a visit to the European Solidarity Centre, it is recommended to allocate sufficient time to fully immerse yourself in the exhibitions and participate in guided tours.
Check the Centre's schedule for any special events, lectures, or cultural programs that may enhance your experience.

The European Solidarity Centre in Gdańsk transcends the role of a traditional museum; it is a vibrant hub of remembrance, reflection, and inspiration.
As visitors walk through its halls, they become witnesses to a chapter

in history where ordinary individuals united to defy oppression and pave the way for a new era of freedom.
The Centre stands as a beacon of solidarity, echoing the timeless message that collective action and the pursuit of justice can shape a brighter future for all.

ARTUS COURT

Artus Court (Dwór Artusa) is located in Gdańsk's Old Town and showcases the city's rich history, architectural splendor, and commercial heritage. This Renaissance-style structure has been a meeting place for merchants, officials, and cultural groups for centuries, making it an iconic landmark that transports tourists back in time. Discover the romantic attraction and historical importance of Artus Court in Gdańsk.

Artus Court, established in the late 14th century and renovated in the 16th century, is a stunning example of Renaissance architecture. The façade is embellished with beautiful sculptures, ornamental themes, and detailed craftsmanship that represent the artistic and cultural influences of the era. The building's façade is a visual symphony of grandeur, evoking a bygone period.

Artus Court has historically served as a gathering place for Gdańsk's rich merchants. Merchants from the Hanseatic League, a medieval commercial association, met here for significant debates, negotiations, and festivities. Artus Court's splendor reflected Gdańsk's bustling trade hub.

Artus Court's Renaissance Courtyard is a tranquil retreat that takes visitors to the elegant Renaissance era. The courtyard is enclosed by arched galleries, has a central well, and is flanked by beautiful arcades, making it an intimate setting that resonates with historical whispers.

The Main Hall (Great Hall) at Artus Court is a remarkable example of Renaissance splendor. The hall, lavishly furnished with wooden panels, tapestries, and elaborate carvings, hosted sumptuous dinners, celebrations, and cultural activities. The ambiance oozes regality, allowing visitors to envisage the enormous festivities that formerly took place inside its confines.

Artus Court is known for its Amber Cabinets, which showcase exquisite amber antiques and jewelry. Gdańsk has a long history of producing and trading amber, as shown by these cabinets. The Amber Cabinets give a dimension of cultural relevance to Artus Court.

Artus Court has served as a cultural and social focus for centuries, in addition to its commercial purpose. The structure featured concerts, dramatic events, and literary elite meetings. Gdańsk's status as a hub of creative and intellectual interaction stemmed from its robust cultural life.

Artus Court showcases sculptures, paintings, and antiques from Gdańsk's cultural and commercial heritage. Visitors may see the elegant furnishings, period costumes, and historical artifacts that represent the city's diverse background.

To get the most out of your visit to Artus Court, consider taking a guided tour to learn about its history and architecture. Check the schedule for any special events or exhibits taking place in the building. Exploring Artus Court throughout the day and evening provides unique views of its ageless beauty.

Artus Court in Gdańsk exemplifies the city's Renaissance beauty, wealth, and cultural life. Wandering through its halls, admiring architectural features, and absorbing historical tales, you'll be transported to a period when Gdańsk was not just a commercial port but also a vibrant cultural and intellectual hub. Artus Court is a living witness to a city's lasting soul, having woven its past into the very fabric of its architectural masterpieces.

AMBER MUSEUM

Gdańsk, a city rich in nautical heritage, serves as an entrance to the fascinating world of Amber. The Amber Museum (Muzeum Bursztynu) in Gdańsk showcases the city's strong connection to the golden jewel. Housed in a historic structure, the museum takes visitors on a fascinating trip into the origins, workmanship, and cultural importance of amber. Let us tour the Amber Museum and discover the fascination of this beautiful petrified resin.

The Amber Museum is situated in Gdańsk's Old Town on Długa Street, which has medieval gothic architecture. The Uphagen House, the museum's physical structure, provides a touch of historical elegance to the experience. The mood is set against a background of cobblestone walkways and colorful buildings, providing an ideal environment for exploring Amber's fascinating history.

The museum offers an in-depth look at the geological origins and development of amber. Amber, a fossilized resin derived from ancient trees, often encompasses flora and wildlife, resulting in a one-of-a-kind time capsule spanning millions of years. Visitors learn about the many forms of amber and the scientific elements of its formation.

The museum's story highlights the cultural relevance of amber in the Baltic area. Amber, often known as "Baltic Gold," plays an important role in local mythology, customs, and handicrafts. The exhibitions demonstrate how amber has been utilized for ages in art, jewelry, and as a symbol of prosperity and protection.

The Amber Museum has an impressive collection of amber

artworks and jewelry. The exhibitions include unique amber carvings, sculptures, and jewelry created by experienced artists. The museum showcases the progression of amber workmanship, from classic designs to modern displays of creative brilliance.

The museum's main feature is the replica of the famed Amber Room. The original Amber Room, built in the 18th century, was lost during WWII. The Amber Museum's replica, created by talented artisans, enables visitors to marvel at the grandeur of this mythical room, which is covered with amber, gold leaf, and precious stones.

The Amber Museum promotes hands-on exploration via

interactive displays and activities. Visitors may participate in activities such as amber polishing, which will let them appreciate the skill required to convert raw amber into wonderful objects. Workshops also provide insight into the craft of amber jewelry creation.

The museum explores the scientific and technical elements of amber. Exhibits examine the use of amber in medicine, research, and the extraction of ancient DNA, demonstrating its importance beyond its aesthetic and cultural value.

The exhibit highlights the historical significance of amber trading routes and its economic value. Amber has been a valuable commodity throughout history, uniting civilizations and developing trade links.

Before leaving, browse the museum store for a chosen assortment of amber jewelry, relics, and gifts. Visitors to the store may take home a piece of the Baltic's luminous treasure, whether it's a one-of-a-kind amber creation or a book on the fascinating world of amber.

To improve your experience at the Amber Museum, consider guided tours and seminars. Check the museum's schedule to see if there are any special exhibits or activities. Photography is often permitted, enabling you to capture the splendor of the exhibitions.

The Amber Museum in Gdańsk is a mesmerizing journey into the world of amber. From its geological origins to its cultural importance, the museum reveals the varied fascination of this golden treasure. As you walk through its exhibitions, you'll discover not just the beauty of amber, but also a deep respect for its significance in defining the Baltic region's cultural and artistic character. Discover the secrets and wonders of Gdańsk's Amber Museum, which will leave you with a renewed appreciation for this ancient treasure.

CHAPTER 6

CULINARY DELIGHTS

TRADITIONAL POLISH CUISINE

Gdańsk's historic charm and marine influences provide a delicious trip into the heart of Polish cuisine. Gdańsk's bustling gastronomic scene highlights traditional Polish cuisine with strong tastes and a combination of Eastern European culinary traditions. From pierogi to substantial stews, the city's restaurants and cafes provide a rich tapestry of tastes that represent Poland's cultural and culinary traditions.

Pierogi, or dumplings, are a must-try while exploring Polish cuisine. These delicious dumplings come in a variety of fillings, including pork, potato, cheese, and sauerkraut. at Gdańsk, you may have pierogi at elegant restaurants or at local markets, where sellers offer them hot and freshly cooked.

Żurek is a classic Polish soup that contains sour rye broth, potatoes, sausage, and hard-boiled eggs. Żurek, a cozy food served in bread bowls, is a favorite option among both residents and tourists.

Bigos, also known as hunter's stew, is a substantial and savory meal that combines sauerkraut, meats (such as sausage, pig, and game), and fragrant spices. Bigos slow-cooked to perfection, is a delicious delicacy that embodies Polish cuisine's strong and complex tastes.

Kotlet Schabowy (Polish Schnitzel): Kotlet Schabowy is a popular Polish meal that consists of a breaded and pan-fried pork cutlet. This meal, served with mashed potatoes and cabbage or salad, captures the basic but delightful spirit of Polish home cuisine.

Stuffed cabbage rolls, known as gołąbki, are a traditional Polish dish that showcases the skill of home cooking. Cabbage leaves are stuffed with a flavorful blend of ground pork, rice, and spices and cooked in a tomato-based sauce. This cozy meal is a mainstay of traditional Polish family gatherings.

Kompot is a gently sweetened and pleasant fruit compote that pairs well with meals. Kompot, made from a variety of dried or fresh fruits, is a popular beverage in Poland, providing a refreshing and hydrating alternative to the heartiness of traditional Polish cuisine.

Finish your gastronomic tour with a piece of Sernik, a Polish cheesecake. Unlike its American cousin, Polish cheesecake is often prepared with farmer's cheese and has a rich and creamy texture. Fruit, chocolate, or a sprinkling of powdered sugar are all possible variations.

Gdańsk is famed for its traditional Polish gingerbread biscuits, Pierniki, which have been prepared for decades. These spicy delicacies come in a variety of shapes and sizes and are sometimes decorated with complex patterns. They make wonderful keepsakes or delicious treats to pair with a cup of tea.

Explore Gdańsk's local markets and street food booths. Here, you may try regional delicacies such as smoked salmon and handmade bread, for a more genuine and relaxed eating experience.

Gdańsk's gastronomic environment, steeped in traditional Polish cuisine, encourages tourists to experience the rich tastes that have created the country's culinary legacy. The city provides a variety of foods that embody the flavor of Polish home cuisine, from pierogi at a local cafe to the soothing warmth of a bowl of Żurek. Dining in Gdańsk takes you on a gastronomic journey that not only feeds your body but also immerses you in the city's rich cultural heritage.

GDAŃSK'S LOCAL SPECIALTIES

Gdańsk, a city steeped in maritime history and cultural variety, provides a gourmet trip that is as varied as its architectural legacy. Gdańsk's unique specialties showcase the city's maritime influences, historical trading links, and robust culinary traditions from Northern Poland. Discover the gastronomic delights that make Gdańsk a food lover's paradise.

Plated Salmon:
Gdańsk, a seaside city, has a vibrant seafood sector, including Łosoś z Platera, a local delicacy that displays the finest of the Baltic Sea. Smoked salmon is often served on a tray with garnishes such as dill, lemon, and horseradish. The salmon's subtle, smoky aromas are an ideal introduction to Gdańsk's seaside culinary delights.

Ryba po Kaszubsku, Kashubian-style. Fish: Kashubia, a region near Gdańsk, has a culinary effect on the city, and Ryba po Kaszubsku is a lovely representation of this link. This meal consists of fish, usually herring or cod, cooked in a unique Kaszubian sauce made with onions, sour cream, and a dash of mustard. The ultimate product is a balanced combination of tastes that honors the local culinary tradition.

Fried herring, known as Smażony Śledź, is a popular dish in Gdańsk, a city known for its marine cuisine. Herring is often coated in seasoned flour, pan-fried till golden, and eaten with potatoes or toast. It's a simple yet tasty meal that embodies the spirit of traditional Baltic cuisine.

Zupa Rybna, or fish soup, is a soothing and hearty meal that represents the city's maritime history. This savory soup, made with a variety of fish, vegetables, and fragrant herbs, is generally served with a dollop of sour cream and a sprinkling of freshly chopped dill. It's a comforting meal, particularly during the winter months.

Gdańska Marynarka, or Gdańsk Navy Rum, is a unique native spirit that honors the city's naval past. This cocktail, made with Caribbean and African rums, spices, and herbs, celebrates Gdańsk's maritime history. Enjoy it straight or as a vital element in local cocktails.

Ciasto Francuskie, often known as French pastry, is a popular sweet dessert in Gdańsk. Layers of flaky pastry are filled with thick custard or fruit compote, resulting in a delicious treat that goes well with a cup of coffee. Gdańsk's sweets are a reflection of the city's history and culinary mix.

Napoleonka, a Polish pastry, has a particular position in Gdańsk's dessert repertoire. This tiered pie has puff pastry sheets interspersed with creamy custard, providing a lovely tactile contrast. It is a popular option for both residents and tourists looking for a sweet treat.

Gdańsk has a growing craft beer sector, with local brewers offering a varied range of beers to suit different preferences. Whether you choose a traditional pilsner, a hoppy IPA, or a deep stout, Gdańsk's native beers provide a refreshing complement to the city's gastronomic delights.

Gdańsk's local markets, such as Hala Targowa and Stary Kleparz, provide handcrafted items and traditional specialties. These markets in Gdańsk provide a diverse range of foods, including regional cheeses, smoked salmon, and artisan chocolates.

Gdańsk's native specialties combine marine traditions, regional influences, and the city's history to create a unique culinary experience. Exploring Gdańsk's culinary scene is not just a gourmet joy, but also a voyage through the city's historic and maritime past.

POPULAR RESTAURANTS AND CAFES

Gdańsk's rich history and energetic environment make it both a visual joy and a gastronomic heaven. The

city's eating scene is a multifaceted tapestry of tastes, blending traditional Polish cuisine with current culinary innovation.
Gdańsk has a diverse range of dining alternatives, from cozy cafes to sophisticated restaurants, to suit every taste. Let's look at some of the prominent restaurants and cafés that add to the culinary charm of this wonderful city.

Restaurants:

1. Restauracija Kubicki: Restauracja Kubicki, located in the center of Gdańsk's Old Town, is a historical jewel from 1918.
Known for its exquisite decor and cuisine that features traditional Polish foods with a modern touch.

Signature meals include pierogi with a variety of fillings, Baltic herring, and delicious pork loin.

2. Piwna 47 Restaurant and Pub: Nestled in the picturesque Piwna Street, this restaurant offers a pleasant pub atmosphere as well as broad food.
Serves substantial dishes such as classic Polish stews, grilled meats, and tasty pierogi.
A diverse assortment of craft brews enhances the dining experience.

3. Gdańsk Restaurant: Gdańska Restaurant, overlooking the Motława River, is well-known for its gorgeous location and panoramic views.
The cuisine combines regional delicacies, such as fresh Baltic fish,

savory soups, and locally produced meats.
Outdoor seating is a fantastic way to enjoy the waterfront scene.

4. Grand Cru Restaurant: Grand Cru, located in the historic Gdańsk Shipyard, provides an elite dining experience focused on contemporary European cuisine.
The restaurant is well-known for its large wine list, which pairs well with its gourmet meals.
The exquisite decor and excellent service make it a popular option for special events.

Translating as "Under the Salmon," this restaurant in the center of the Old Town is a seafood lover's dream.
The restaurant specializes in Baltic seafood dishes, such as the popular

Łosoś z Platera (Platter of Salmon) and fish soups.
The warm environment and nautical-themed décor improve the eating experience.

Cafés:

1. Literacka Café. Literacka Café, located in a historic tenement building, offers bohemian appeal and a literary atmosphere.
The café is a sanctuary for coffee connoisseurs, serving a selection of gourmet brews with fresh pastries and treats.
Cozy nooks and book-lined shelves offer a welcoming environment for rest and discussion.

2. Cafe Ferber: Café Ferber, near the Motława River, offers delicious pastries and stunning views.

Provides a diverse array of coffee concoctions, as well as a delectable collection of cakes, pastries, and gourmet sandwiches.
During the warmer months, the terrace with views of the river is a popular option.

3. Gdańska Manufaktura Czekolady: Gdańska Manufaktura Czekolady is a chocolate store and café, making it a chocolate lover's delight. Indulge in handcrafted chocolates, hot chocolate beverages, and desserts made with premium cocoa. The comfortable environment and the fragrance of chocolate make it an ideal spot for a sweet pause.

4. Café liberté: Café Liberté, located in the center of the Old Town, is a trendy café with modern decor and a lively environment.

The menu includes a variety of coffees, teas, and inventive drinks, as well as light meals and snacks. The stylish atmosphere makes it a popular destination for both residents and visitors.

5. Kawiarnia Kamienica: Kawiarnia Kamienica, located in a historic tenement building, has a nostalgic appeal with its old décor and comfortable atmosphere.
Serves a variety of coffees, teas, and freshly baked goodies, including traditional Polish pastries.
The cozy atmosphere and courteous personnel make this a great place to have a relaxing coffee break.

Gdańsk's culinary culture combines history with innovation, providing a varied range of eating options for both residents and tourists. Gdańsk's famous restaurants, whether serving pierogi in a historic restaurant or a cup of coffee in a pleasant café, enrich the city's cultural tapestry. From the Old Town's cobblestone alleyways to the picturesque coastline, each eating establishment adds to the culinary allure of this enchanting coastal city.

STREET FOOD SCENE

Gdańsk's vibrant street food culture exemplifies the city's dynamic energy. As you walk through the old alleyways and along the picturesque shoreline, you'll come across a variety of intriguing street food options that showcase the distinct tastes of Polish and Baltic cuisine. Gdańsk's street food sellers provide a variety of savory and sweet delights, adding to the city's culinary diversity.

1. Zapiekanka Stalls: Zapiekanka is a popular Polish street meal that consists of an open-faced baguette covered with melted cheese, mushrooms, and other tasty toppings.
Zapiekanka stalls may be found in several areas, including the famed Plac Dominikański, providing a fast and tasty snack for both residents and visitors.

2. Obwarzanki Stands: Obwarzanki are ring-shaped bread treats that are similar to bagels but with a distinct Polish twist. They are often

sprinkled with sesame seeds, poppy seeds, or salt.
Look for stalls around prominent locations like the Gdańsk Shipyard or along Ulica Długa, where merchants offer freshly baked obwarzanki in various flavors.

3. Smakołyki Rybne (fish snacks): Given Gdańsk's nautical past, the street food scene contains excellent fish nibbles, including grilled or smoked fish on a stick.
Vendors along the coastline and at local markets sell a variety of seafood, enabling you to enjoy the tastes of the Baltic Sea while on the move.

4. Grilled Kielbasa (Sausage) Stands: Experience the seductive fragrance of grilled kiełbasa floating across the streets. Polish

sausages are a popular street dish in Gdańsk, recognized for their savory and smokey taste profiles. Grilled kielbasa, eaten on a bun or with a side of mustard, is a popular and pleasant street food alternative.

5. Pączki, or doughnuts: Polish doughnuts, pączki, are available in a variety of tastes and fillings. Look for local bakeries or street food vendors that provide these wonderful delicacies, which are sometimes sprinkled with powdered sugar or glazed to perfection.

6. Jarmużne Smakołyki (Pierogi Truck): Look for food trucks or booths that provide unique pierogi fillings and preparations for a

contemporary take on classic pierogi.
These mobile pierogi restaurants often provide several alternatives, enabling you to enjoy this traditional Polish delicacy in a new and innovative manner.

7. Fruit and Juice Stands: Stay hydrated with the availability of fresh fruits and liquids sold at street kiosks.
On warm days, Gdańsk's streets offer a variety of nutritious and tasty options, including seasonal berries and freshly squeezed citrus drinks.

8. Chłodnik (Cold Soup) vendors: During warmer months, vendors may sell chłodnik, a pleasant cold soup with beets, cucumbers, and yogurt.

This distinctive and vibrant soup is both nutritional and invigorating, making it an ideal street food alternative on a sunny day.

The street food scene in Gdańsk offers a diverse culinary experience. Street food sellers in Gdańsk provide a variety of savory and sweet options, including grilled sausages, open-faced baguettes, doughnuts, and inventive pierogi. As you tour the city's streets and attractions, don't miss out on the various and scrumptious street food selections that add to the vivid energy of this coastal treasure.

CHAPTER 7

SHOPPING IN GDAŃSK

MAIN SHOPPING STREETS

Gdańsk, a city steeped in history and culture, provides scenic landscapes, architectural wonders, and a thriving commercial scene. Gdańsk's major retail streets provide a variety of stores, boutiques, and traditional markets, attracting both residents and visitors. Explore some of Gdańsk's most popular shopping streets and experience the city's retail appeal.

Długa Street is one of Gdańsk's most recognizable and busy thoroughfares. This cobblestone boulevard, which runs from the

Golden Gate to the Green Gate, is studded with beautiful ancient buildings that house a variety of businesses, cafés, and restaurants. Visitors may browse a variety of local and worldwide brands, including clothes and accessories as well as one-of-a-kind souvenirs. Długa Street hosts seasonal markets and cultural events, making it a vibrant retail destination year-round.

Mariacka Street offers an elegant atmosphere and a look at Gdańsk's amber past. This quaint cobblestone lane, known for its handmade amber businesses, has lovely houses and wrought-iron balconies. Explore boutique boutiques that specialize in fine amber jewelry, which is frequently created by experienced local artists.

Mariacka Street offers a one-of-a-kind shopping experience, with each object telling a narrative, making it a great destination for people looking for unique mementos.

St. John's Street, also known as Ulica Świętojańska, showcases Gdańsk's historic splendor. This street is lined with stores, cafés, and historic buildings, providing a combination of classic and contemporary shopping experiences. Discover local workmanship at charming shops, where handcrafted handicrafts and regional products highlight the city's cultural diversity. St. John's Street also has hidden jewels like antique shops and bookshops, making it an ideal location for anyone with diverse preferences.

Long Market (Długi Targ) is the major plaza of Gdańsk's Old Town and a thriving commercial area. This old market area is surrounded by beautiful homes and has a variety of stores and vendors. Visitors may visit local markets, where sellers sell fresh food, homemade crafts, and regional delicacies. Long Market is also filled with trendy boutiques and souvenir stores, making it a great location for leisurely shopping while taking in the city's bustling ambiance.

Świętopełk Street, surrounded by ancient buildings, provides a unique and calm shopping experience. This lovely boulevard is home to boutique shops, art galleries, and quiet cafés. Strolling along Świętopełk Street, you may discover unusual fashion items, handcrafted handicrafts, and modern art. The quiet setting and diverse offers make it an ideal location for people who like finding hidden gems away from the masses.

The major retail streets in Gdańsk provide a unique shopping experience that combines history, culture, and local character. Whether you're looking for high-end apparel, handcrafted crafts, or unusual souvenirs, the city's diversified retail environment guarantees a fascinating and stimulating shopping experience for every visitor. Explore the streets of Gdańsk to experience the city's unique retail culture.

AUTHENTIC SOUVENIRS

bGdańsk, a city steeped in history and nautical culture, provides a treasure trove of original souvenirs reflecting its rich cultural past. Explore local markets and boutique shops to bring home a piece of Gdańsk's distinctive character, including amber jewelry and traditional crafts. Let's explore the world of genuine gifts that capture the essence of this wonderful Baltic city.

Amber jewelry, sometimes known as the "Gold of the North," has a rich historical and cultural significance in Gdańsk. Gdańsk is known for its superb amber artistry, and the city's streets are lined with jewelry stores displaying this fossilized resin. Authentic gifts often feature handmade amber necklaces, bracelets, and earrings, each of which tells a Baltic Sea narrative. Visitors may stroll along Mariacka Street, which is known for its amber artists, to discover one-of-a-kind creations that capture the beauty of this rare gemstone.

St. Mary's Basilica, a prominent landmark in Gdańsk, has inspired local artisans to make unique souvenirs. Look for finely created objects like paintings, prints, and sculptures that highlight the majestic architecture of this famous cathedral. These creative interpretations create fascinating and culturally interesting mementos, bringing a bit of Gdańsk's skyline into your house.

Explore traditional Polish ceramics as a memento to immerse yourself in the country's artistry. Gdańsk has stores selling traditional Polish ceramics with colorful colors and elaborate designs. Plates, bowls, and mugs include folk-inspired themes that represent the country's creative legacy. These utilitarian and artistically beautiful products serve as both distinctive and practical gifts that capture the spirit of Polish heritage.

Authentic handwoven fabrics are ideal for showcasing regional craftsmanship. Shops in Gdańsk sell traditional Polish textiles such as scarves, shawls, and blankets. Look for products made of natural fabrics and embellished with regional designs to provide a comfortable and genuine feel to your souvenir collection.

Baltic Sea-inspired Crafts: Gdańsk's nautical heritage has led to an abundance of Baltic Sea-inspired souvenirs. Handcrafted ship models, nautical-themed jewelry, and sea-inspired home décor are popular options. These distinctive souvenirs honor the city's maritime traditions and serve as charming recollections of your stay in Gdańsk.

Authentic souvenirs from Gdańsk provide a real link to the city's rich history and cultural tapestry. From the warm colors of amber jewelry to the complex designs of traditional pottery, each memento offers a story about the Baltic area. Explore local markets, handmade stores, and lovely streets to find genuine gifts to beautify your house and serve as treasured memories of your time in Gdańsk.

LOCAL MARKETS AND BOUTIQUES

bGdańsk's rich maritime heritage and dynamic cultural landscape provide a pleasant shopping experience via local markets and attractive stores. Exploring the city's marketplaces and shops offers a unique chance to find one-of-a-kind treasures, ranging from traditional crafts to modern designs. Discover the best shopping destinations in Gdańsk for original and different experiences.

Hala Targowa, Gdańsk's medieval Market Hall, is a thriving hive of activity. Located in the middle of the city, this indoor market has a variety of vendors offering fresh fruit, meats, cheeses, and local specialties. Dive into the bustling atmosphere as both residents and visitors browse the market's numerous products. Hala Targowa offers authentic Gdańsk cuisine, including selected fruits and regional delicacies. Experience Gdańsk's culinary legacy by interacting with merchants, sampling local delights, and discovering unusual items to take home.

Gargamel Vintage & Retro Shop is a must-see shop for vintage aficionados and retro fashion lovers. Located on Świętopełk

Street, this quirky boutique provides a chosen range of vintage apparel, accessories, and décor items. Explore shelves loaded with one-of-a-kind items, ranging from classic apparel to eccentric accessories, allowing you to add a touch of nostalgia to your wardrobe or home.

Błękitny Wieżowiec, often known as the Blue Tower, is located in Gdańsk's Old Town and has stores showcasing local designers and craftspeople. This sophisticated shopping destination combines current clothes, artisan crafts, and elegant home décor. Błękitny Wieżowiec offers a variety of shops, each with a unique personality, making it a popular destination for visitors seeking to support local talent and discover the current trends.

Ulica Artystyczna, often known as Artistic Street, has stores and galleries showcasing local craftsmanship. This pedestrian-friendly boulevard is lined with colorful facades, providing a pleasant background for your shopping trip. Explore businesses that sell handcrafted jewelry, art prints, and one-of-a-kind souvenirs created by local artisans. Ulica Artystyczna combines creativity and commerce to provide a unique shopping experience that captures the creative character of Gdańsk.

Łosoś i Czosnkowa is a Gdańsk-based specialty store that offers a carefully chosen assortment of high-quality culinary goods. This store caters to sophisticated palates, offering handmade cheeses and charcuterie as well as premium wines and chocolates. Łosoś i Czosnkowa offers a taste of the region's culinary quality, making it an ideal gift for foodies.

Gdańsk's local markets and shops provide a variety of shopping experiences, from visiting old market halls to uncovering hidden jewels in contemporary retail areas. Gdańsk offers many shopping options, including fresh local products, vintage apparel, modern design, and handmade delights. Explore the city's picturesque streets, mingle with local merchants, and discover the treasures that make Gdańsk's markets and shops a shopper's paradise.

CHAPTER 8

NIGHTLIFE AND ENTERTAINMENT

BARS AND PUBS

Gdańsk's dynamic nightlife scene includes a variety of taverns and pubs to suit all tastes. Gdańsk offers a diverse range of dining choices, including specialty drinks, local breweries, and quiet pubs. Join us on a tour of the city's top bars and pubs, each with its distinct charm and character.

Piwnica Rajców, located in Gdańsk's Old Town, is a historic bar built in a 14th-century edifice. Piwnica Rajców is popular among both residents and visitors, because of its medieval atmosphere and vast beer variety, which includes both local breweries and foreign favorites. The pub's subterranean setting, replete with brick arches and wooden tables, provides a pleasant and appealing ambiance for those wishing to spend a relaxing evening with friends.

Brovarnia Gdańsk is a must-visit for beer fans looking to sample local beers. This microbrewery, located in the historic Granary Island neighborhood, mixes the craft of brewing with a trendy pub atmosphere. Enjoy a variety of specialty beers made on-site, as well as a menu that combines traditional Polish cuisine with a contemporary touch. The outdoor patio with views of the Motława

River enhances your drinking experience.

Literacka, located on Piwna Street, combines literature, art, and specialty drinks to create a unique dining experience. This literary-themed pub has shelves full of books and a cuisine inspired by great works. Sip masterfully made cocktails named after literary works while immersing yourself in the warm and intellectual atmosphere. Literacka offers a stylish and diverse atmosphere for individuals who want to enjoy both cocktails and books.

Kokomo, located in the center of Gdańsk, offers a tropical experience in the city. This Caribbean-inspired pub in Old Town is well-known for its relaxed environment, bright design, and unique beverages. With a menu featuring a variety of rum-based drinks and fresh fruit concoctions, Kokomo provides a refreshing escape from the bustling city streets. This pub offers a tropical escape without leaving Gdańsk, including live music and a lively audience.

Piękny Pies: If you're in the mood for live music and a bohemian vibe, Piękny Pies (Beautiful Dog) is the place to be. This legendary Gdańsk pub, located on Chlebnicka Street, has been a cultural hub for artists and musicians for decades. Enjoy a relaxed ambiance, interesting design, and a broad assortment of drinks while listening to live music ranging from jazz to rock. Piękny Pies is more than a tavern; it's a cultural institution that embodies Gdańsk's free spirit.

Gdańsk's bars and pubs provide a broad and vibrant nightlife experience for all tastes and preferences. Whether you're seeking historic charm, craft beers, literary inspiration, tropical vibes, or live music, Gdańsk has a venue to suit every mood.
Embrace the city's lively spirit, raise a glass in one of its unique establishments, and savor the eclectic flavors of Gdańsk's vibrant nightlife.

LIVE MUSIC VENUES

Gdańsk has a vibrant live music scene that reflects the city's cultural vitality. Gdańsk has a diverse range of music venues, from ancient to small, exhibiting both established and upcoming acts. Join us as we discover the city's live music venues, where harmonizing notes from diverse genres come to life.

Klub Zak, located on Długi Targ Street in Gdańsk's Old Town, is a well-known live music venue. Klub Zak, located in a historic building with exposed brick walls and an intimate atmosphere, has been a popular music venue since the 1980s. The facility features a wide variety of acts, including rock, jazz, blues, and alternative music. Klub Zak is a popular live music venue in Gdańsk, known for its unique atmosphere and focus on promoting local and international talent.

B90, located on Granary Island, is a flexible cultural facility that changes into a vibrant music venue in the evening. The theater has both indoor and outdoor stages, which provide a dynamic environment for live events. B90 features performances of diverse genres, including indie, electronic, rock, and hip-hop. B90's modern design and dynamic surroundings make it an ideal setting for exceptional live music performances.

The Shakespeare Theatre in Gdańsk is not only known for its theatrical productions but also for hosting live music events. This unusual venue, built in a renovated medieval structure, features events ranging from classical and chamber music to modern and experimental sounds. The Shakespeare Theatre stands out for its historic atmosphere and superb acoustics, making it an ideal location for people looking for a refined live music experience.

Wydział Remontowy, situated on historic Stolarska Street, is a popular live music venue noted for its alternative and indie music scene. Wydział Remontowy's relaxed ambiance, exposed brick walls, and eccentric design appeal to a wide range of music aficionados. The venue features both local and traveling musicians, resulting in an intimate location where listeners may interact with developing artists in a more personal setting.

Protokultura, located in Gdańsk Wrzeszcz, is a cultural institution and live music venue that promotes variety. Protokultura caters to a diverse spectrum of musical preferences, including indie, punk, techno, and experimental. The facility also organizes art exhibits, film screenings, and community activities, making it a lively and welcoming location for both artists and visitors.

Live music venues in Gdańsk combine historic elegance with modernity. Gdańsk offers a variety of musical experiences, from nostalgia-filled bars to sophisticated cultural spaces and intimate alternative venues. Discover Gdańsk's vibrant music scene, where creative artists and enthusiastic audiences collaborate to produce remarkable experiences.

CULTURAL EVENTS AND FESTIVALS

Gdańsk, a city rich in history and culture, hosts several cultural events and festivals throughout the year. Gdańsk provides a variety of events for both inhabitants and tourists, including traditional holidays and modern arts presentations. Explore Gdańsk's cultural calendar to discover the exciting events and festivals that make it a cultural hotspot.

The St. Dominic's Fair (Jarmark Dominikański) is a popular summer event in Gdańsk that kicks off the season. This colorful fair, which dates back to the 13th century, fills the alleys of the Old Town with a brilliant assortment of vendors, performances, and cultural events. Visitors may discover local crafts, eat regional cuisines, and watch live music and street entertainment. Every August, thousands of people go to Gdańsk for the St. Dominic's Fair, which celebrates the city's nautical heritage.

The Gdańsk Shakespeare Festival is a cultural highlight for those interested in theater. This yearly festival brings together theatrical groups from across the globe to commemorate William Shakespeare's timeless works. Performances take place in a variety of locations across the city, including the famous Shakespeare

Theatre. The Gdańsk Shakespeare Festival provides a broad and engaging theatrical experience, including traditional interpretations and creative adaptations.

Gdańsk Music Festival (Music Festival in Gdańsk):
The Gdańsk Music Festival, an annual event for classical music enthusiasts, features prominent performers and ensembles. The festival, which takes place in historic settings such as St. Mary's Basilica and the Oliwa Cathedral, has a series of performances with classical works and modern interpretations. The Gdańsk Music Festival showcases classical music for both local and international audiences.

The Open'er Festival, held in Gdańsk, is one of Poland's most well-known music events. The Gdynia-Kosakowo Airport, located near Gdańsk, hosts a multi-genre music event with notable international and Polish musicians. Open'er Festival has a diversified roster that appeals to a wide spectrum of musical preferences, including rock, pop, electronic, and hip-hop. The festival's exciting atmosphere and worldwide reputation make it a must-see for music fans.

The Gdańsk Dance Festival is an annual event that showcases contemporary dance groups from Poland and beyond. The festival offers a wide schedule of performances, seminars, and talks, fostering creative interaction and research. The Gdańsk Dance Festival offers unique and thought-provoking dance works in various venues across the city, making it a must-attend for everyone interested in movement and expression.

Gdańsk's cultural events and festivals showcase the city's rich history, inventiveness, and diversity. Gdańsk offers many cultural experiences, including medieval fairs, classical music, and music festivals. Gdańsk's cultural character is woven together via its vibrant schedule of events and festivals.

GDAŃSK BY NIGHT

Gdańsk's Old Town transforms when the sun sets, bringing the city's wonderful spirit to life at night. The lit facades, bustling streets, and a plethora of entertainment choices create a welcoming environment for both inhabitants and tourists. Join us as we discover Gdańsk's midnight charm.

Długi Targ and Długa Street, located in Gdańsk's Old Town, become more appealing at night. The ancient facades of colorful townhouses are attractively lighted, offering a stunning setting for a nighttime promenade. The street is lined with attractive cafés, restaurants, and bars, each giving a nice area to sip a drink and take up the atmosphere. Długa Street is a great place to start an evening in Gdańsk, with street performers adding a magical touch to the atmosphere.

The Motława River Embankment reflects lights from riverbank facilities, providing a magnificent environment. Riverside cafés and restaurants provide outdoor seating with views of the lit Gdańsk Crane and other sights. Enjoy a leisurely nighttime boat on the river to see the city lights from a fresh viewpoint, or relax at one of the waterfront locations to enjoy the quiet beauty of Gdańsk.

Amber Sky Rooftop Bar offers a panoramic view over Gdańsk at night. Perched atop the Radisson Blu Hotel, this modern bar provides stunning views of the city skyline, including the historic St. Mary's Basilica and Old Town. Sip handmade cocktails or enjoy a bottle of wine while seeing the magnificent city lights below. The rooftop location adds class to your evening, making it an excellent choice for a romantic night out or a celebratory drink.

Piwna Street is a popular nightlife destination with a vibrant ambiance. Piwna Street is lined with taverns, restaurants, and live music venues, providing a vibrant evening experience. Join residents and other visitors as you explore the broad selection of enterprises, each with its distinct charm. Piwna Street offers a diverse range of options for a fun night out in Gdańsk, including traditional pubs serving local beers and fashionable cocktail establishments.

Long Market Square (Długi Targ) is a popular meeting spot at night, with gentle lighting illuminating the Neptune Fountain and Green Gate. The square's cafés and restaurants flow out into the cobblestone walkways, providing a vibrant setting for outdoor dining and mingling. Gdańsk's historic plaza is a beautiful combination of history and modernity, perfect for a nightcap beneath the stars.

Exploring and celebrating in Gdańsk by night offers a unique blend of history and modern appeal. Gdańsk after dark offers a remarkable and enchanting experience, whether wandering along old streets, having a drink with a view, or immersing in the active nightlife.

CHAPTER 9

OUTDOOR ACTIVITIES

RELAXING ON GDAŃSK BEACHES

Gdańsk is known for its rich history and active city life but also provides a calm respite along its gorgeous coastline. Gdańsk's beaches along the Baltic Sea provide a relaxing refuge with sun-soaked coastlines and peaceful waves. Join us as we explore the peaceful beaches of Gdańsk, allowing you to relax and enjoy the beauty of the coastal scenery.

Sopot Beach, located a short rail trip from Gdańsk, is a popular location for residents and visitors. This sandy beach stretches for many kilometers along the Baltic Sea, providing plenty of area for sunbathing, beach activities, and long, leisurely walks. The unique wooden pier that extends into the sea offers breathtaking views of the coastline and acts as a focal point for guests looking for a peaceful vacation by the ocean.

Stogi Beach, located in the eastern section of Gdańsk, offers a calmer and less crowded choice for people seeking peace. The sandy beaches are flanked by dunes and pine trees, providing a natural refuge away from the rush and bustle of the city. Stogi Beach is noted for its clean and well-kept surroundings, making it a great site for a calm day of sunbathing, reading, or just relaxing to the soothing sound of waves.

Brzeźno Beach, situated in northern Gdańsk, is a popular family getaway with a large sandy beach and shallow seas. The beach is surrounded by colorful beach bungalows, which give attractiveness to the coastal backdrop. Visitors may participate in a variety of water activities or enjoy a leisurely walk along the promenade, where cafés and ice cream stalls provide delicious refreshments with a view of the sea.

Jelitkowo Beach, located between Sopot and Brzeźno, is a relaxing length of shoreline. Jelitkowo Beach, with its excellent golden sand and clean seas, offers a quiet location for sunbathing and enjoying the Baltic Sea air. The beach is well-equipped with amenities such as beachfront eateries and rental services for beach chairs and umbrellas, offering a pleasant and peaceful stay.

Westerplatte Beach offers a unique beach experience with historical value. Located on the famous Westerplatte Peninsula, this beach provides a calm getaway and an insight into Gdańsk's wartime past. Visitors may enjoy the sun and water while also seeing neighboring sights such as the Westerplatte Monument and the relics of the Military Transit Depot.

Gdańsk's beaches provide a peaceful respite from the city's

busy streets, ideal for anyone seeking leisure and natural beauty. Whether you like the bustling ambiance of Sopot Beach or the peaceful beaches of Stogi, Gdańsk's coastal scenery encourages you to relax and bathe in the sun, enjoying the tranquil rhythm of the Baltic Sea. Discover the unique coastal charm that enhances Gdańsk's cultural and natural offers.

PARKS AND GARDENS

Gdańsk, a city recognized for its historical beauty, has a magnificent tapestry of parks and gardens that give a calm getaway from the urban chaos. Gdańsk's green areas provide a relaxing connection with nature, whether for a leisurely walk, a family picnic, or a quiet time. Join us as we visit the parks and gardens that provide a sense of calm to the urban.

Oliwa Park (Park Oliwski) is a beautiful green oasis in the Oliwa area, known for its historical importance and lovely scenery. The park surrounds the Oliwa Cathedral and has charming walks, ponds, and finely designed gardens. Visitors may explore the Abbots' Palace's ancient architecture, relax with the calming sounds of the Oliwa Stream, and see the centuries-old trees that give shade on hot summer days. Oliwa Park is not only a nature lover's paradise, but it also serves as a cultural getaway with open-air concerts and art exhibits.

The Gdańsk Shakespeare Garden (Ogród Szekspirowski) is a pleasant and small green spot in the Old Town, inspired by the works of the legendary playwright. The garden has Elizabethan-style flowerbeds, medicinal gardens, and statues portraying Shakespearean characters. The Gdańsk Shakespeare Garden, with its quiet environment and vistas of ancient buildings, provides a lovely respite for literature enthusiasts and those seeking a tranquil break inside the city center.

Park Jelitkowski, located near the shore in the Jelitkowo area, provides a peaceful environment with stunning coastline views. The park is popular among residents and tourists looking for a pleasant day outside. Park Jelitkowski, with its walking pathways, playgrounds, and expansive lawns, is an excellent location for family picnics, leisurely bike rides, or a quiet time by the sea. The park's closeness to the shore enhances the overall natural splendor of the experience.

Ronald Reagan Park (Park Im. Ronalda Reagan): Ronald Reagan Park, named after the United States' 40th President, is a contemporary urban park in the Wrzeszcz area. The park has a modern design, interactive exhibits, and colorful green areas. Ronald Reagan Park, with its playgrounds, exercise facilities, and dedicated picnic sites, provides opportunities for both active leisure and relaxation. The park's well-kept landscape attracts both locals and tourists looking to see Gdańsk's different districts.

Park Ołowianka, located on Ołowianka Island, provides a peaceful getaway with water views. This waterfront park offers breathtaking views of the Motława River and the old buildings of Gdańsk. Visitors may take a leisurely walk along the riverside, rest on chairs viewing the water, or spend a peaceful period among the flora. Park Ołowianka offers a peaceful retreat near Gdańsk's prominent monuments.

The parks and gardens of Gdańsk combine nature and culture to provide relaxing and rejuvenating environments for both inhabitants and tourists. Gdańsk's green spaces, including Oliwa Park,

Shakespeare Garden, and Ronald Reagan Park, provide natural beauty to match the city's history.

BOATING AND WATER SPORTS

Gdańsk's gorgeous coastline and proximity to the Baltic Sea attract water lovers seeking exhilarating boating and water sports activities. Gdańsk provides a variety of water sports and cruises along the coast to suit your preferences. Join us in exploring Gdańsk's aquatic playground, a popular destination for boaters and water sports aficionados.

Gdańsk's strategic position on the Baltic Sea makes it a popular destination for sailing aficionados.

The city provides a variety of sailing excursions, including private boat charters and sailing schools for those who want to learn the ropes. Set sail from Gdańsk Marina to enjoy the splendor of the Baltic Sea, including cool winds and breathtaking coastline vistas. Whether you're an experienced sailor or a beginner, Gdańsk's waterways provide a thrilling environment for a nautical adventure.

Explore Gdańsk from a fresh viewpoint while kayaking along the gorgeous Motława River. Several rental firms in Gdańsk provide kayaks for peaceful paddling or guided trips around the historic Old Town. Paddle beneath renowned bridges, past ancient buildings, and beside vibrant waterfront cafés to immerse yourself in the city's marine feel while enjoying the tranquility of the river.

Jelitkowo Beach, situated in northern Gdańsk, is a renowned windsurfing location. The large sandy beach and constant breezes make it an excellent location for windsurfing experiences. Whether you're an experienced windsurfer or a novice seeking instruction, Jelitkowo Beach offers a dynamic setting for riding the waves and experiencing the pleasure of this thrilling water activity.

Gdańsk provides water skiing and wakeboarding for thrill seekers. Visit one of the water sports facilities along the coast, where professional instructors may walk you through the fundamentals or help you improve your abilities. Experience the thrill of being towed behind a boat and slicing through the waves, creating amazing memories on the Baltic Sea.

Enjoy a relaxing aquatic adventure with a canal cruise or boat trip around Gdańsk's canals. Explore the Motława River and its canals by boat, taking in the city's ancient architecture. Gdańsk's marine beauty may be enjoyed via themed cruises, sunset excursions, and dinner cruises offered by different operators.

The waterways of Gdańsk provide a variety of boating and water sports opportunities for both explorers and aficionados. Gdańsk offers a diverse range of marine activities, including windsurfing, kayaking along the river, and sailing on the Baltic Sea. Immerse yourself in the city's nautical flair, where the natural beauty of the ocean serves as a dramatic background for unique aquatic excursions.

CYCLING ROUTES

Gdańsk, a city rich in history and surrounded by beautiful scenery, welcomes cyclists to explore its streets and scenic routes. Cycling aficionados may combine urban exploration with natural beauty, seeing the city's historic sites, beautiful neighborhoods, and waterfront views. Explore Gdańsk's cultural legacy and natural beauty via varied bike routes.

Cycle along the Royal Route (Trakt Królewski) to explore the history of Polish kings. The route begins at the ancient Green Gate in the Old Town and leads riders past the majestic Artus Court, Neptune Fountain, and Długi Targ, exhibiting the architectural beauty of Gdańsk's Golden Age. Continue towards the Oliwa neighborhood, passing past the Oliwa Cathedral and Park, and enjoy the royal splendor of this bicycle path.

The Coastal Cycling Trail in Zatoki Gdańskiej provides a scenic ride along the Baltic Sea. Begin at Gdańsk and continue the well-marked track down the seashore, passing via Sopot and Gdynia. Take in the sea wind, see the panoramic views of the Baltic, and visit attractive beach communities along the route. The Coastal Riding Trail combines nautical beauty with the thrill of riding.

Follow the Granaries on Motława River Trail to enjoy cycling and waterfront views. Begin at the Green Gate in Old Town and cycle down the Motława River to see Gdańsk's old granaries and warehouses, now turned into museums, galleries, and cafés. The path provides a unique perspective on the city's nautical past while also offering a fun route for bicycles to visit the riverfront sights.

Gdańsk Hills Trail (Trasa Wzgórz Gdańskich) offers a demanding cycling ride through the scenic Gdańsk Hills. This walk leads you through the Tricity Landscape

Park's forested landscape, including hills, woods, and picturesque overlooks. Starting in the Oliwa neighborhood, bikers may explore the Tricity Landscape Park and its network of paths, which provide a nature-filled retreat inside the city boundaries.

Explore Gdańsk's historical importance by cycling along the Westerplatte Peninsula Trail. Begin your adventure in the city center and ride to Westerplatte, the location of the first World War II combat. Cycle through the beautiful environs, past monuments, and remains of military history. The route combines natural beauty with a meaningful link to Gdańsk's history.

Gdańsk's bicycle routes are suitable for bikers of all abilities, from relaxed urban exploration to tough terrain and historical landscapes. Gdańsk's numerous routes provide a unique combination of architectural wonders, nautical charm, and natural beauty, making it a popular cycling destination. So take your bike, breathe in the fresh air, and let the wheels guide you around the charming streets and paths of this old Polish city.

CHAPTER 10

DAY TRIPS FROM GDANSK

SOPOT: THE RIVIERA OF THE BALTIC SEA

Nestled along the Baltic Sea's shoreline, Sopot is a gem on the Tricity coast, presenting a unique combination of coastal beauty, historic elegance, and bustling cultural life. Sopot, located near Gdańsk and known as the Riviera of the Baltic Sea, is a popular tourist attraction with sandy beaches, a famous pier, and a vibrant atmosphere. Join us as we explore the charm of Sopot, a seaside hideaway that flawlessly blends leisure and entertainment.

Sopot is known for its distinctive wooden pier, which is the longest in Europe and extends gently into the Baltic Sea. The 511-meter-long pier encourages tourists to promenade across the water, taking in panoramic views of the coastline, enjoying the sea wind, and catching the spirit of Spots nautical attractiveness. At the pier's end, an antique lighthouse provides a nostalgic touch to the gorgeous ocean.

Monte Cassino Street, the major promenade of Sopot, has a dynamic and bohemian vibe. The street, lined with attractive cafés, shops, and art galleries, is a bustling center of activity both day and night. Stroll along the cobblestone pathways, browse the quirky stores, and get a coffee or a meal at one of the street-side restaurants. Monte Cassino Street comes alive in the evenings with a vibrant nightlife, making it a hub for socializing and entertainment.

Sopot Beach: This gorgeous sandy beach spans along the coastline and offers a sun-soaked paradise for beachgoers. The beach is separated into parts that serve diverse needs, ranging from family-friendly areas to those perfect for water sports aficionados. Visitors may rest on beach loungers, swim in the Baltic Sea, or participate in beach volleyball and windsurfing. Sopot Beach is not only a relaxing destination, but it also serves as a location for a variety of events and festivals held along the beach.

Sopot's old buildings are well-preserved, adding to the city's architectural appeal. The Grand Hotel, a 1920s architectural jewel, exemplifies Sopot's exquisite history. The ancient Kurhaus, with its unique green dome, is another renowned structure that has seen the town's social and cultural life for a century. Sopot's architecture, which combines Art Nouveau and antique styles, gives the Baltic Sea Riviera a timeless charm.

Sopot Forest (Las Sopocki) offers a natural retreat inside the town. This wide woodland area has walking and cycling routes, making it a peaceful escape for nature lovers. The forest's meandering pathways lead to vantage spots with panoramic views of Sopot and the surrounding terrain, making it a great location for a calm escape from the seaside crowds.

Sopot, known as the "Riviera of the Baltic Sea," offers a wonderful combination of beach peacefulness, historical elegance, and bustling cultural activity. This coastal jewel provides a variety of activities, whether you're taking a leisurely walk down the wooden pier, discovering the bohemian ambiance of Monte Cassino Street, or relaxing on the sun-kissed sands of Sopot Beach. Discover the enchantment of Sopot, where the Baltic Sea meets timeless elegance to create a location that captures the hearts of all who come.

MALBORK CASTLE

Malbork Castle, a UNESCO World Heritage Site and one of the most important medieval monuments in Europe, rises magnificently along the Nogat River near Gdańsk. This enormous red-brick stronghold, known as the Grand Fortress of the Teutonic Order, depicts the narrative of medieval chivalry, military skill, and the intriguing history of the Teutonic Knights. Join us as we discover the enthralling story of Malbork Castle, a symbol of medieval beauty near Gdansk.

Malbork Castle, built in the 13th century, housed the Teutonic Knights, a medieval military order dedicated to defending Christianity in the Holy Land. Over the ages, the castle grew into a strong fortress, modifying its look and architecture. The castle was an important point in the region's history, experiencing battles, sieges, and political changes.

Malbork Castle is an architectural marvel that showcases medieval workmanship and military engineering. The castle has three primary sections: the High Castle, the Middle Castle, and the Low Castle. The High Castle, with its tall walls and watchtowers, functioned as the Grand Master's home and administrative headquarters for the organization. The knights lived in the Middle Castle, while the Low Castle housed the castle's personnel, stables, and workshops.

The interiors of Malbork Castle include Gothic art and ornamental features. The castle's Great Refectory, with its ornate vaulted ceilings and stained glass windows, provides an insight into the medieval lifestyle of the Teutonic Knights. The great Master's Palace, a Gothic architectural marvel, has elaborate rooms, a chapter house, and a great hall that hosts sumptuous dinners and celebrations.

Malbork Castle has an impressive collection of amber items, highlighting the region's historic trading history. The Amber Museum on the castle grounds showcases amber objects ranging from little trinkets to complex jewelry. The exhibitions give information about the artistry and importance of amber in the medieval Baltic area.

Malbork Castle is both a historical landmark and a cultural hub. The castle organizes a variety of activities, such as medieval reenactments, concerts, and exhibits, where visitors may immerse themselves in bygone ages. Special displays inside the castle delve into many facets of its history, art, and the Teutonic Order's effect on the area.

Malbork Castle is a stunning example of medieval architecture and the Teutonic Knights' rich history. Visit this UNESCO World Heritage Site in Gdańsk for a captivating voyage through time. Explore the towering walls, complex interiors, and cultural richness of one of Europe's most spectacular medieval strongholds. Malbork Castle invites history buffs, architectural aficionados, and inquisitive visitors alike to explore the majesty and heritage of a bygone period along the banks of the Nogat River.

HEL PENINSULA

The Hel Peninsula, located north of Gdańsk, is a tiny strip of land that gently extends into the Baltic Sea. The Hel Peninsula, known for its clean beaches, picturesque fishing towns, and nautical charms, provides a peaceful respite from metropolitan life. Join us as we explore this unique coastal treasure, where land meets the horizon to create an exquisite spot near Gdańsk.

The Hel Peninsula, a 34-kilometer-long isthmus between the Bay of Puck and the Baltic Sea, offers a breathtaking coastal landscape. The peninsula's scenery is defined by undulating dunes, windswept pine woods, and magnificent beaches that run along both sides of the continent. Visitors are met with panoramic views of the sea and bay, offering a magnificent environment for leisure and exploration.

The Hel Peninsula has lovely beach villages with distinct atmospheres and access to gorgeous coastlines. Popular destinations such as Jastarnia and Jurata draw tourists with their sandy beaches, coastal promenades, and a wide range of water sports activities. The resorts provide a wonderful balance of coastal quiet and contemporary conveniences, making them ideal for anyone looking for a beachside getaway.

The Hel Peninsula is a dream destination for water sports aficionados. The peninsula's exposed position delivers steady winds, making it an excellent choice for windsurfing and kitesurfing. The shallow waters near the bay are ideal for sailing and kayaking, while the open sea provides an exciting setting for more daring pursuits. Water sports schools and rental facilities serve both novices and experienced enthusiasts, guaranteeing that everyone can enjoy the marine playground.

The Hel Peninsula has lovely fishing communities, including Hel and Jastarnia, with traditional wooden homes and antique lighthouses that add to the region's marine beauty. Explore the local fishing culture, taste fresh seafood at local restaurants, and visit the Fisheries Museum in Hel to learn about the area's rich marine heritage. The settlements symbolize the peninsula's residents' eternal relationship to the sea.

The Help Seal Sanctuary in the Bay of Puck is a must-see for nature enthusiasts. The sanctuary is devoted to the conservation of seals, namely the common and gray seals that live in the Baltic Sea. Visitors may watch these lovely marine creatures in their natural environment and hear about conservation efforts to protect the local seal population.

The Hel Peninsula, located north of Gdańsk, offers a quiet vacation with beautiful beaches, picturesque settlements, and nautical beauty. The Hel Peninsula provides a broad selection of activities, whether you want to relax by the sea, participate in water sports, or learn about the region's rich nautical heritage. Immerse yourself in the coastal splendor of this exquisite continent, where the Baltic horizon meets the sandy coastlines, resulting in a location that captures the hearts of everyone who visits.

KASHUBIAN SWITZERLAND

Nestled in the embrace of northern Poland, Kashubian Switzerland unfolds as a serene and picturesque region, offering a tranquil retreat just a short distance from Gdańsk. Renowned for its rolling hills, lush forests, and charming lakes, Kashubian Switzerland invites nature lovers, hikers, and seekers of peaceful landscapes to immerse themselves in its pristine beauty. Join us as we explore this hidden gem, where the natural allure of the landscape captivates the soul.

Scenic Landscapes and Rolling Hills: Kashubian Switzerland earns its moniker with a landscape reminiscent of Switzerland's rolling hills and verdant meadows. The region is characterized by gentle slopes, scenic valleys, and dense forests, creating a picturesque setting for those seeking an escape into nature. The changing hues of the landscape throughout the seasons add to the region's enchanting appeal, making it a year-round destination for outdoor enthusiasts.

Kashubian Ethnographic Park: Immerse yourself in the rich cultural heritage of the Kashubian people at the Kashubian Ethnographic Park (Kaszubski Park Etnograficzny) in Wdzydze Kiszewskie. The open-air museum showcases traditional Kashubian architecture, including historic wooden cottages, windmills, and other structures. Visitors can explore the park, gaining insight into the region's history, craftsmanship, and the unique way of life of the Kashubian people.

Wdzydze Kiszewskie Lake District: The Wdzydze Kiszewskie Lake District is a captivating feature of Kashubian Switzerland, comprising a chain of interconnected lakes surrounded by lush forests. The lakes, including Wdzydze, Gołuń, and Radolne, offer opportunities for boating, fishing, and leisurely lakeside strolls. The tranquility of these crystal-clear waters provides a perfect escape for those seeking a peaceful connection with nature.

Szymbark: Center of Kashubian Culture: Szymbark, a village at the heart of Kashubian Switzerland, serves as a cultural hub where visitors can delve into Kashubian traditions and craftsmanship. The famous "Upside Down House" (Dom do Góry Nogami) is a quirky attraction, challenging perceptions with its inverted interior. The village also hosts events, festivals, and craft fairs that celebrate Kashubian art, music, and culinary traditions.

Przywidz: A Gateway to Nature: Przywidz, located at the edge of Kashubian Switzerland, acts as a gateway to the region's natural wonders. Surrounded by forests and hills, Przywidz is an ideal starting point for hiking and cycling adventures. Explore the trails that wind through the landscape, providing breathtaking views of the countryside and an opportunity to connect with the pristine beauty of Kashubian nature.

Kashubian Switzerland, with its rolling hills, serene lakes, and cultural richness, stands as a peaceful retreat near Gdańsk. Whether you're exploring traditional Kashubian architecture, enjoying the tranquility of the lake district, or hiking through the scenic landscapes, the region captivates with its natural beauty and cultural heritage. Kashubian Switzerland invites travelers to escape the urban hustle and immerse themselves in the calming embrace of this hidden gem, where the spirit of Kashubia comes alive amid the captivating tapestry of nature.

CHAPTER 11

PRACTICAL TIPS AND LOCAL INSIGHT

SAFETY AND HEALTH

Prioritizing safety and health during your trip to Gdańsk is crucial for a relaxing and enjoyable experience. Gdańsk, like any other city, provides a combination of historical richness, cultural variety, and contemporary conveniences. Being aware of safety precautions and healthcare services is vital. Discover how to be safe and healthy when exploring Gdańsk.

Emergency Services: Gdańsk, like every modern city, has a reliable emergency service system. In an emergency, call 112 for help. This number links you to standard emergency services, such as police, fire, and medical aid. The operators are fluent in English, facilitating clear communication during crises.

Gdańsk has contemporary healthcare facilities such as hospitals, clinics, and pharmacies to provide tourists with necessary medical services. Major hospitals in the city, such as the University Clinical Centre (Uniwersyteckie Centrum Kliniczne), provide extensive medical services. Furthermore, pharmacies (apteki) are distributed across the city, selling a variety of over-the-counter pharmaceuticals and healthcare supplies.

immunizations & Health Precautions: Before coming to Gdańsk, make sure regular immunizations are up-to-date. Consider immunizations for infections like hepatitis A and B, and see your healthcare professional for specific recommendations depending on your health and travel plans. Simple measures, such as maintaining excellent cleanliness and being hydrated, may improve your general well-being throughout your vacation.

Gdańsk, like many European towns, has rigorous food and water safety requirements. However, you must dine at recognized restaurants and make sure your meat and fish are fully cooked. In Gdańsk, tap water is normally safe to drink. However, bottled water is available at numerous shops and supermarkets.

Personal Safety: Gdańsk is noted for its low crime rates compared to other European cities. However, regular safety measures apply. Keep a watch on your goods in busy situations, utilize dependable transportation, and be alert to your surroundings. While the city is typically safe to explore, use common sense to ensure a safe and pleasant trip.

Stay up-to-date on COVID-19 criteria and limits while the worldwide epidemic continues. Gdańsk and other localities may have particular safeguards in place to minimize the spread of the virus. To ensure a safe visit, follow local legislation, practice proper hygiene, and keep informed about testing and vaccine alternatives.

Gdańsk welcomes tourists and offers a diverse range of cultural and historical activities. You may completely enjoy your visit to this interesting city by putting safety and health first. To guarantee a safe and pleasurable voyage through Gdańsk's magnificent surroundings, observe these suggestions whether visiting the Old Town, wandering through the streets, or relishing local cuisine.

COMMUNICATION TIPS

To really enjoy your visit to Gdańsk, it's important to communicate well. While English is frequently spoken in tourist locations, knowing a few essential words and cultural subtleties will help you communicate with people and enjoy your stay more. Discover Gdańsk-specific communication techniques to connect with the city and its people.

Learn basic Polish phrases: While English is widely spoken in Gdańsk, people appreciate tourists who make an effort to communicate in Polish. Learning a few fundamental words may help you connect with others more easily. Simple pleasantries, such as "Dzień dobry" (Good morning), "Proszę" (Please), and "Dziękuję" (Thank you), are courteous and warmly accepted.

Polish culture prioritizes politeness and formality, particularly in early meetings. Using "Pan/Pani" (Mr./Mrs.) to address someone you don't know well is considered courteous. As the discussion progresses, you may be asked to use first names, but beginning with formal titles is a gracious approach.

linguistic translation applications may provide on-the-go linguistic support. These tools may help you translate text and even enable voice chats. While English is widely spoken, having a translation software may be especially useful in locations where English is not as prominent.

Be aware of nonverbal cues: Nonverbal communication is a crucial part of human contact that differs by culture. Maintaining eye contact is valued in Gdańsk as a show of honesty and connection. Additionally, a warm handshake is a typical greeting, particularly in business or professional contexts.

Understanding cultural norms in Gdańsk may improve communication due to the city's rich history. Poles may seem reserved at first, but once a connection is made, talks become warm and interesting. Taking a real interest in local customs and traditions creates a good environment.

When utilizing public transportation, it's important to know crucial Polish vocabulary like "bilet" (ticket) and "przystanek" (bus/tram stop) in addition to

English signs. Public transit employees often know English, so don't be afraid to ask for help if necessary.

Participating in local events, trips, or activities allows you to engage with locals. Cultural festivals, guided tours, and local markets all provide natural settings for conversation. Locals are typically eager to share their expertise and experiences with tourists.

To communicate effectively in Gdańsk, it's important to grasp cultural subtleties that enhance relationships beyond language. These communication ideas can help you connect with the heart of Gdańsk and make your stay unforgettable. They include employing simple Polish words, being careful of nonverbal clues, and connecting with the local population. Experience Gdańsk's cultural richness and welcoming atmosphere.

SUSTAINABLE TRAVEL PRACTICES

We can help preserve Gdańsk's cultural and natural assets by making responsible travel choices. Embracing sustainable travel habits not only enriches your personal experience but also guarantees that the city's beauty is preserved for future generations. Join us to explore ethical and eco-friendly travel options in Gdańsk.

Choose Eco-Friendly Accommodations: Look for places

that value sustainability. Look for hotels and guesthouses that promote energy conservation, trash reduction, and environmentally friendly methods. By supporting environmentally responsible businesses, you help to further the city's overall commitment to sustainable tourism.

Gdańsk's efficient public transportation system, comprising buses and trams, lowers carbon emissions compared to private automobile usage. Consider taking public transit to explore the city. Furthermore, Gdańsk is a bicycle-friendly city with designated pathways. Renting a bike or going for a stroll not only decreases your carbon footprint but also enables you to immerse yourself in the local environment.

Support small businesses and craftspeople to promote local culture and economy. Choose local restaurants that stress locally produced products, and visit markets that sell handcrafted items. This allows you to help local communities while also reducing the environmental effects of mass-produced items.

Respect Cultural legacy: Responsible tourism requires respect for Gdańsk's rich historical and cultural legacy. Follow established walkways, avoid handling artifacts, and consider the historical value of sites. Participate in guided tours given by expert residents who may provide information about the city's history and legacy.

Reduce and Reduce single-use plastic use. Bring a reusable water bottle and refill it at specified stations. Say goodbye to single-use plastics like straws and bags, and instead choose eco-friendly alternatives. Minimizing plastic trash helps preserve Gdańsk's beautiful environment.

Maintain proper waste management practices throughout your stay in Gdańsk. Use recycling bins for recyclable materials and rubbish disposal containers. Participate in local projects or beach cleaning activities, if applicable, to help the city maintain a clean and sustainable environment.

To save energy and resources, switch off lights and electronics when not in use. Help to save water by using towels and linens sensibly. Adopting eco-friendly practices helps lessen your environmental effects and coincides with Gdańsk's dedication to sustainability.

Learn about local conservation efforts and consider getting involved. Many organizations and community initiatives in Gdańsk prioritize environmental conservation, historical preservation, and sustainable development. Supporting or participating in these programs immediately benefits the city and its surroundings.

Sustainable travel patterns in Gdańsk contribute to conserving the city's cultural and natural heritage. By making thoughtful decisions, from your lodging to your everyday activities, you become a vital part of the city's sustainable tourism initiatives. Explore Gdańsk responsibly, making a good influence on the community and environment. We can guarantee that Gdańsk remains a treasured destination for future generations of tourists.

LOCAL ETIQUETTE

Gdańsk's rich history and varied culture emphasize the importance of local etiquette in encounters. Embracing the subtleties of Polish culture improves your experience and develops strong relationships with locals. Learn about Gdańsk etiquette to negotiate social situations with elegance and cultural knowledge.

Polish culture places great importance on politeness, and greetings are an important part of social interactions. When meeting someone for the first time or in formal contexts, a handshake is customary. Use the proper titles, such as "Pan" for Mr. and "Pani" for Mrs., until you are asked to use first names. It is usual to say "Dzień dobry" (Good morning) or "Dobry wieczór" (Good evening) when entering a room or beginning a discussion.

Polish etiquette emphasizes personal space and respect. Maintain a comfortable distance during chats and avoid making physical contact unless you have a close connection with the individual. It is usual to wait for others to complete speaking before offering your comments, displaying tolerance for opposing viewpoints.

When welcomed to someone's house, it is customary to offer a little gift, such as flowers or chocolates, as a show of thanks. When delivering a gift, it is usual to use both hands. If you get a present, open it in front of the giver as a gesture of appreciation. Polish hospitality is warm and generous, so expect to get invited to dinners and parties.

Polish eating etiquette emphasizes formality, particularly in formal settings. Wait for the host or hostess to begin the meal, and use the correct utensils. Keep your hands on the table, but not your elbows. It's also polite to finish everything on your plate, signaling that you liked the meal.

Cultural sensitivity is vital in Gdańsk. Avoid controversial issues like politics and religion unless the discussion organically takes that path. Poles may take some time to warm up in social circumstances, but patience and a genuine interest in their culture may go a long way toward developing relationships.

Dressing correctly demonstrates respect in Polish culture. When visiting churches or attending formal occasions, dress modestly and avoid casual clothing. In daily contexts, clean and well-presented attire is preferred.

Language & Communication: While English is frequently spoken, particularly in tourist regions, learning basic Polish words is encouraged. Locals generally enjoy it when outsiders try to speak their language. Use "Proszę" (Please) and "Dziękuję" (Thank you) as customary courtesies in everyday encounters.

Tipping is prevalent in Poland, and service costs are not usually included in restaurant bills. In restaurants, it is typical to tip about 10-15% of the whole amount. Tipping is also prevalent in taxis, hotels, and other services.

Understanding local manners in Gdańsk might enhance your vacation experience. Embracing local traditions, greetings, and social standards demonstrates respect for the local culture and fosters deep ties with the Gdańsk community. Remember that a genuine interest in the city's customs and traditions will improve your entire experience and leave you with lasting memories of your visit to this lovely place.

CHAPTER 12

ACCOMMODATION GUIDE

HOTELS IN VARIOUS BUDGET RANGES

Gdańsk, a city with a rich history and active cultural scene, caters to a varied variety of guests, providing hotels for all budgets. Gdańsk offers a variety of hotels to suit your needs, including luxury, mid-range comfort, and budget-friendly alternatives. Join us as we visit hotels at various price points, ensuring that every traveler finds the ideal home away from home in this beautiful Polish city.

Luxury hotels:

Hotel Gdańsk, located along the Motława River in the heart of the Old Town, is a five-star property that blends historical elegance with contemporary luxury. The hotel has nicely designed rooms, a spa, and magnificent views of the city. The central position allows visitors to quickly explore Gdańsk's historic sights while enjoying the comfort of luxury rooms.

PURO Gdańsk Stare Miasto is a design-focused luxury hotel located near the major train station. It offers a fashionable refuge in the city center. The hotel has modern décor, cutting-edge services, and a rooftop patio with spectacular views. PURO values sustainability, making it a perfect alternative for environmentally conscientious tourists seeking luxury.

Mid-range Hotels:

Located in Gdańsk's Old Town, Holland House Residence combines traditional grandeur with contemporary comfort. The hotel's rooms are decorated in a classic style, and visitors can enjoy facilities such as a spa center and a rooftop terrace. Its central position makes it ideal for visiting the city's attractions on foot.

Hanza Hotel, overlooking the Motława River, offers a superb position and mid-range price. The hotel has modern rooms, a restaurant that serves Polish cuisine, and a patio with spectacular river views. Hanza Hotel is an ideal starting point for exploring Old Town since it is close to the medieval crane and other sights.

Budget-Friendly Options:

Hostel Kwadrat provides budget-friendly but comfortable accommodations. Located in the Wrzeszcz neighborhood, the hostel offers clean and comfortable dormitory-style accommodations. Hostel Kwadrat is a good alternative for individuals looking for a low-cost, social stay.

Amber Hostel, located near the Main Town Hall in Gdańsk's Old Town, offers affordable and convenient lodging options. The hostel has dormitory-style accommodations and modest facilities, making it a great alternative for backpackers and budget tourists who want to immerse themselves in the historic beauty of Gdańsk.

Gdańsk has a variety of hotels to fit any traveler's interests, including luxury, mid-range comfort, and budget-friendly options. These hotels in Gdańsk embody the city's distinctive character and hospitality, offering both historic Old Town charm and contemporary design-focused areas for a pleasant stay.

HOSTELS AND GUESTHOUSES

Gdańsk, a city famed for its historical beauty and energetic environment, welcomes guests of all types, including those seeking affordable lodgings. Hostels and guesthouses in Gdańsk provide a pleasant and social setting, making them excellent for backpackers, lone travelers, and those seeking an immersive experience in the center of the city. Join us in exploring the pleasant hostels and guesthouses in Gdańsk.

Hostel Cycle On, located in the trendy Wrzeszcz neighborhood, offers affordable bicycle-themed accommodations. The hostel provides dormitory-style accommodations with an emphasis on environmentally friendly methods. With its shared kitchen, warm common spaces, and bicycle rental service, Hostel Cycle On fosters a friendly and convivial environment for guests.

Amber Hostel, conveniently situated near the Main Town Hall in Gdańsk's Old Town, offers a budget-friendly and outstanding location. The hostel offers dormitory-style accommodations, providing affordability while preserving the city's historic character. The shared kitchen and common rooms provide a welcoming environment in the center of Gdańsk.

Grand Hostel Gdańsk, located in a historic tenement house in the Old Town, provides affordable and comfortable accommodations. The hostel offers a range of accommodation types, including individual rooms and dorms, all decorated in a contemporary style. The hostel's central position allows visitors to conveniently explore Gdańsk's prominent sights while also enjoying the public areas.

La Guitarra Hostel Gdańsk, located in the Old Town, offers a comfortable and creative accommodation choice. The hostel's vivid design, helpful staff, and social spaces add to the lively environment. Whether sleeping in shared dormitories or individual rooms, travelers may experience Gdańsk's creative and cultural environment.

Dom Muzyka provides a cultural guesthouse experience with comfortable accommodations in a historic structure in the city center. The Gdańsk Music Academy operates this guesthouse, which offers a peaceful respite with well-appointed rooms and a beautiful garden. It is a good alternative for guests wanting a calmer setting while being near Gdańsk's attractions.

Villa Pica Paca, situated in the Wrzeszcz neighborhood, offers contemporary conveniences while maintaining the elegance of a guesthouse. The property has uniquely furnished rooms, a garden, and a comfortable sitting space. Villa Pica Paca offers a welcoming environment for travelers visiting Gdańsk.

Hostels and guesthouses in Gdańsk serve a varied variety of guests, giving both affordability and a distinctive and social experience.

Whether you prefer the historic ambiance of the Old Town or the bustling atmosphere of Wrzeszcz, these lodgings offer a welcome retreat for visitors wishing to immerse themselves in the cultural tapestry of Gdańsk while remaining affordable.

UNIQUE STAYS AND BOUTIQUE ACCOMMODATIONS

Gdańsk provides unique and boutique hotels for guests looking for an outstanding experience. These places blend excellent design, customized service, and a unique atmosphere to produce unforgettable stays. Discover Gdańsk's unique stays and boutique hotels, each with its tale to tell.

Hotel Podewils in Gdańsk is a beautifully renovated 18th-century granary beside the Motława River, offering timeless elegance and historical charm. This boutique hotel in the center of Old Town has uniquely designed rooms with antique antiques and contemporary facilities. Guests may take in the lovely riverfront views and have excellent meals at the hotel's gourmet restaurant.

Hanza Hotel Gdańsk, located on the waterfront with breathtaking views of the Motława River, flawlessly combines contemporary luxury with nautical tradition. The boutique hotel offers modern rooms, some with exposed brick walls and nautical-inspired décor. Guests may relax in the sauna, eat eastern regional cuisine in the hotel restaurant, and enjoy the unique ambiance of Gdańsk's waterfront.

Dom Aktora (Actor's House) is a boutique guesthouse located in Gdańsk's Old Town, providing a unique creative getaway. Each room in this 16th-century structure is named after a well-known Polish actor, making for a memorable and immersive visit. Dom Aktora's warm and beautifully renovated rooms allow guests to explore the historic richness of the Old Town while also relaxing.

Hotel Haffner, located in Sopot, a beach resort town near Gdańsk, provides a boutique retreat with contemporary and luxury touches. The hotel has a modern design, big rooms, and a wellness facility overlooking the Baltic Sea. Guests may enjoy spa treatments, exquisite restaurants, and the bustling environment of Sopot.

Gotyk House, a historic Gothic building in Gdańsk's Old Town, offers cozy and elegant boutique accommodations. The skillfully renovated rooms combine medieval characteristics with contemporary amenities. Gotyk House's prime position enables tourists to see Gdańsk's rich history and architectural splendor.

Radisson Blu Hotel Gdańsk provides a boutique experience on the Motława River, combining contemporary design with nautical tradition. The hotel's modern decor is enhanced by breathtaking views of the Old Town and the landmark Gdańsk Crane. Guests may enjoy upmarket facilities, such as a rooftop patio with magnificent city views.

Gdańsk's unique stays and boutique lodgings improve the notion of hospitality, allowing guests to immerse themselves in the city's history, culture, and modern allure. Gdańsk's lodgings, ranging from old granaries with river views to imaginatively decorated guesthouses in the Old Town, provide a unique and rewarding experience that enhances the pleasure of touring the city.

CHAPTER 13

TRANSPORTATION GUIDE

PUBLIC TRANSPORTATION

Gdańsk's rich history and dynamic cultural scene make it a fascinating place to visit. Fortunately, the city has a well-connected and efficient public transit system, making it simple for travelers to traverse its picturesque streets and see diverse sites. Join us for a complete guide to public transit in Gdańsk, helping you make the most of your visit to this interesting Polish city.

The tram network in Gdańsk is a vital element of the city's public transportation system, offering dependable and convenient travel options. Trams link significant neighborhoods such as the Old Town, Wrzeszcz, and Oliwa. Look for tram stations with a stylized "N" sign. Ticket vending machines are accessible at major stations, and you must verify your ticket upon boarding.

The bus network in Gdańsk complements the tram system by providing service to regions not serviced by trams. Buses are a useful means of transportation for getting to outlying areas and touring outside the city core. Buses, like trams, have ticket-selling machines at key stations, and you must verify your ticket when you board.

SKM (Szybka Kolej Miejska) is an efficient means to travel between Gdańsk and nearby towns. SKM links Gdańsk, Sopot, and Gdynia, creating the Tricity metropolitan region. The railway is a fast and efficient mode of transportation that offers beautiful views of the Baltic Sea as you travel along the coast.

Water trams and ferries provide a unique public transportation option in Gdańsk due to its waterfront position. Water trams run along the Motława River, offering attractive routes connecting Old Town, Westerplatte, and the Shipyard. Ferries link Gdańsk to the beach cities of Sopot and Gdynia, providing a delightful and maritime-inspired excursion.

Ticketing & Fare Information: Gdańsk's public transportation system employs a uniform ticketing system for trams, buses, and the SKM. Single-ride tickets and day passes are available, providing a variety of travel requirements. Tickets may be bought via vending machines at key stops, aboard trams and buses, or through mobile apps. Remember to verify your ticket before or during boarding.

Integration with Gdańsk Card: The Gdańsk Card provides tourists with unlimited public transit for a set duration, making it a convenient and cost-effective option for exploring Gdańsk. Furthermore, the card offers free or cheap admission to a variety of museums and sites, making it a handy choice for travelers.

Accessibility: Gdańsk's public transit system is geared to accommodate those with limited mobility. Many trams and buses have ramps or low floors to make it easier for passengers to embark in wheelchairs or strollers. The official transportation website provides information about accessibility features.

Gdańsk's public transportation network is efficient and diversified, allowing tourists to easily explore the city and its surroundings. Gdańsk's public transit system provides easy access to the city's cultural and natural treasures, whether walking through the ancient alleys of the Old Town or taking a picturesque tram ride along the Baltic Sea.

TAXIS AND RIDE-SHARING

Gdańsk's bustling streets and numerous attractions invite guests to discover its rich cultural tapestry. Several transit choices, like taxis and ride-sharing programs, make getting about the city easier. Whether you're visiting the ancient Old Town, the lively markets, or the picturesque seaside districts, taxis and ride-sharing provide convenient and efficient modes of transportation. Explore Gdańsk's taxi and ride-sharing options in this detailed guide.

Traditional taxis are widely accessible in Gdańsk, offering a convenient and dependable method of transportation. Taxis may be hailed from the street, obtained at authorized taxi stands, or reserved via local taxi firms. Look for certified taxis with readily visible identification, such as a taxi sign and a rate card inside the vehicle. Taxis in Gdańsk use meters to compute rates depending on the distance traveled.

Consider utilizing taxi apps in Gdańsk to make hailing a cab more convenient. Popular applications such as iTaxi and myTaxi enable users to book a cab, monitor its arrival, and even pay using the app. These applications provide clarity in rate calculation, making the taxi experience more convenient for both residents and tourists.

Ride-sharing services have been popular in Gdańsk, providing an alternative to regular taxis. Companies such as Uber exist in the city, enabling customers to order trips using a smartphone app. Ride-sharing services often provide upfront pricing, real-time monitoring of the driver's position, and cashless payments via the app, providing another degree of convenience for passengers.

Taxi stops are strategically positioned around Gdańsk, including transit hubs, prominent sights, and bustling business districts. Cab stands provide an easy and structured approach to immediately locating a cab. Furthermore, these booths often include information on regular charges as well as contact information for local taxi firms.

Taxi fares in Gdańsk are normally metered and dependent on the distance traveled. When you start your travel, be sure the meter is running. Taxi drivers are often acquainted with important landmarks and locations, but giving an address or a detailed description of your destination will assist in guaranteeing a pleasant journey. Tipping is expected, and rounding up the price is normal practice.

Taxis and ride-sharing services in Gdańsk are typically accessible to those with limited mobility. However, it is best to note any special requirements when reserving a trip to verify that the vehicle can accommodate individuals with impairments. Some taxi firms may provide accessible cars on request.

Safety Tips: While cabs in Gdańsk are typically safe, it's important to exercise care. Make sure you only utilize legal and reliable taxi services. Confirm the taxi's identity before getting in, and if you're using a ride-sharing service, double-check the driver's name and the license plate number supplied in the app. If you're concerned about safety, look into well-known taxi stands or reliable ride-sharing services.

Taxis and ride-sharing services in Gdańsk provide a flexible and handy way to explore the city and environs. Gdańsk offers a variety of transportation alternatives, including conventional taxis and ride-sharing applications, for smooth and comfortable travel.

CAR RENTALS

Exploring Gdańsk's ancient neighborhoods, scenic coastline locations, and adjacent regions is a rewarding experience, made even more easy with vehicle rentals. Renting a car allows you to explore the varied landscapes around Gdańsk. This tutorial will explain how to hire a vehicle in Gdańsk and explore the city at your leisure.

Gdańsk has many well-known automobile rental firms that provide a variety of cars to meet diverse travel demands.

International companies like Hertz, Avis, and Europcar operate throughout the city, delivering a consistent and dependable car rental service. Furthermore, smaller businesses provide possibilities for individuals wanting more customized services.

To book a rental vehicle in Gdańsk, you may use major car rental companies' websites or visit their local offices. Many tourists choose to utilize online travel firms that aggregate rental alternatives, enabling them to compare rates and select the finest car for their needs. To obtain the preferred car, reserve ahead of time, particularly during high tourist seasons.

To hire a vehicle in Gdańsk, you must satisfy specific prerequisites.

Most rental organizations require tenants to be at least 21 years old, however this might vary per firm. A valid driver's license, a credit card in the renter's name, and an international driving permit are often needed for non-EU nationals. Familiarize yourself with the rental agency's unique needs.

Gdańsk car rental firms provide a wide selection of vehicles, including tiny cars for city exploration and big SUVs for outdoor activities. When choosing a car, keep your trip party's size, the quantity of baggage, and the kind of terrain in mind. Automatic and manual gearbox choices are often offered.

To drive safely in Gdańsk, it's important to understand local driving restrictions. In Poland, traffic moves on the right side of the road, and seat belts are required for all passengers. The speed restriction varies by kind of route, with metropolitan areas often having a limit of 50 km/h. Stay informed about local traffic laws to guarantee a safe and enjoyable driving experience.

Parking in Gdańsk includes both paid and free zones. Parking places in the Old Town may be limited, and entrance to some locations is restricted. Paid parking is provided in both designated lots and on-street spots. Many hotels also provide parking for visitors. To avoid a citation, follow parking signs and laws.

Fuel stations in Gdańsk and Poland accept major credit cards and are widely dispersed. Petrol stations sell both diesel and unleaded gasoline. It is recommended that you review the fuel policy in your rental agreement to see if you must return the vehicle with a full tank or whether the rental agency charges for refilling.

Car rentals in Gdańsk provide guests with the freedom to explore the city and environs freely. Whether you're planning a gorgeous coastline drive or an excursion to the surrounding Kashubian countryside, a rental vehicle gives you the freedom and convenience you need to make the most of your trip through this interesting part of Poland.

GETTING AROUND ON FOOT

Gdańsk's Old Town, cobblestone streets, and historic monuments make it an ideal city to explore on foot. Walking through the small alleyways and along the gorgeous waterfront enables tourists to immerse themselves in the rich history, lively culture, and architectural marvels that distinguish this Polish treasure. This detailed book explores the joys of walking about Gdańsk, ensuring you don't miss any lovely corners of this enchanting city.

Gdańsk's Old Town is a historical and architectural wonderland that may be explored on foot for a nostalgic experience. Explore Długa Street, filled with vibrant merchant buildings and lively street entertainers. Admire the Gothic grandeur of St. Mary's Basilica and the medieval ambiance of the Main Town Hall. The Old Town's small layout makes it easy to navigate on foot, enabling you to uncover hidden jewels around every corner.

Gdańsk's waterfront promenade offers stunning views of old shipyards, marine museums, and the renowned Gdańsk Crane. The lovely riverfront is lined with cafés and restaurants, providing ideal opportunities to linger, relax, and enjoy the marine atmosphere.

Long Lane (Ulica Długa) is the major street in Gdańsk's Old Town and a pedestrian paradise. Long Lane encourages you to enjoy a leisurely walk through its stately homes, attractive stores, and friendly cafés. The Neptune Fountain, a symbol of Gdańsk, stands proudly at one end of this historic boulevard, with the Green Gate waiting at the other.

Mariacka Street is a must-see for anyone looking to see Gdańsk's jewelry district. This street is famous for its cobblestone pavement and unusual gabled buildings, as well as for its amber businesses. Admire the wonderful amber jewelry on exhibit, and enjoy the enchanting ambiance provided by lantern-lit nights.

Explore the Oliwa Park and Cathedral region, located outside the Old Town. Here, you'll find a beautiful park and the impressive Oliwa Cathedral. Oliwa Park, with its groomed grass and ponds, offers a calm respite. The church, famous for its magnificent organ recitals, is a marvel of Baroque architecture. A stroll around the park and a visit to the church provide a peaceful contrast to the busy city core.

Gdańsk has a variety of public art and sculptures located across the city. The installations on Piwna Street, including the renowned Jacek Mańdziak Bench and the amusing Piwna Street Cats, lend a creative touch to your walking tour. While walking about Gdańsk, keep a look out for these hidden creative jewels.

Explore Gdańsk's history with a guided walking tour.
Knowledgeable guides will take you around the city's highlights, providing intriguing tales and

perspectives. Guided tours provide a systematic and entertaining method to explore the rich history of Gdańsk's streets.

Walking about Gdańsk is a gratifying experience that allows you to explore the city's beauty, history, and cultural diversity at your own speed. Exploring Gdańsk on foot is a magical excursion through ancient lanes, riverbank vistas, and hidden jewels.

CHAPTER 14

GDAŃSK FOR FAMILIES

FAMILY-FRIENDLY ATTRACTIONS

Gdańsk, with its intriguing combination of history, culture, and maritime charm, is not just a destination for adults, but also provides a variety of family-friendly activities catering to young adventurers. Gdańsk welcomes families with wide arms, offering interactive museums and lively parks. In this tour, we will explore the finest family-friendly attractions in Gdańsk, making it a perfect location for memorable excursions with the family.

The European Solidarity Centre, steeped in the city's history, provides an engaging experience for families. The interactive exhibits and multimedia displays give a fascinating glimpse into the history of the Solidarity movement, making it an instructive and entertaining visit for youngsters and teens.

The Gdańsk Science Centre encourages curiosity and fosters a passion for science in young minds. Children may learn about scientific ideas in a fun and engaging way via interactive exhibitions, seminars, and hands-on experiments. The center often conducts educational programs that make learning an enjoyable and family-friendly experience.

Gdańsk Zoo is a great place to spend the day exploring animals. The zoo, which houses a broad assortment of animals such as elephants, giraffes, and penguins, provides a wonderful location for families to explore. Specialized play areas and educational displays guarantee that children enjoy their visit while also learning about the significance of animal protection.

The Museum of Amber, located on Mariacka Street, is a family-friendly attraction. The museum highlights the beauty and importance of amber via interactive exhibits and workshops where children may make their amber-inspired artworks. It's a distinct and informative experience that mixes history, art, and workmanship.

The Hewelianum Centre, named for astronomer Johannes Hevelius, offers interactive scientific and educational experiences. With outdoor exhibitions, a planetarium, and hands-on activities, this facility piques interest in astronomy, physics, and the natural world. The expansive grounds also have a playground, making it an excellent location for family picnics.

Kwiat Paproci (Fern Flower) Playground, located in the Oliwa area, offers a fanciful world for youngsters. The playground's concept is based on Polish culture, namely the mystery of discovering the elusive Fern Flower. With colorful play structures, climbing frames, and slides, this park is a great place for youngsters to burn off energy while parents relax in the beautiful surroundings.

The Baltic Sea Science Center in adjacent Gdynia provides an immersive aquatic experience and is conveniently accessible from Gdańsk. The center's interactive displays include marine life, habitats, and the Baltic Sea. Touch pools and aquariums enable youngsters to get up close to marine animals, making it both informative and exciting.

Sopot, a resort town near Gdańsk, has a stunning sandy beach ideal for family fun and relaxation. Children may make sandcastles, play in the shallow waves, or just enjoy the lively ambiance of the crowded pier. Sopot's bustling streets also include ice cream parlors and cafés catering to family interests.

Gdańsk offers several family-friendly activities for all ages to create unforgettable experiences. The city's numerous offers, which range from educational activities to outdoor excursions, make it a great destination for families looking for the right balance of fun, learning, and discovery. Gdańsk encourages families to experience its beauty and warmth, whether they are exploring history, science, or just relaxing by the sea.

KID-FRIENDLY RESTAURANTS

Gdańsk's numerous eating choices and vibrant culinary scene make it a welcoming destination for families. Exploring the city's restaurants becomes a pleasurable experience when you come across establishments that not only appeal to discriminating palates but also create a welcome environment for young guests. This guide explores the top kid-friendly restaurants in Gdańsk, allowing parents and children to enjoy the pleasures of this attractive Polish city together.

Krowarzywa, a vegetarian and vegan-friendly restaurant near the Main Town Hall, offers healthful and tasty meals. The bright and cheerful design, along with a broad menu that includes plant-based burgers and wraps, make it an enticing option for families. The pleasant personnel and relaxing atmosphere enhance the overall family-friendly experience.

Gdańska Oranżeria, located in Oliwa Park, is a family-friendly restaurant with a scenic location. The menu includes a range of foods ideal for youngsters, and the large outside patio is a beautiful place for families to dine while admiring the verdant surroundings.

Momo Grill in Wrzeszcz is a family-friendly restaurant with a broad menu of grilled dishes. Momo Grill, with its warm and friendly ambiance, welcomes both adults and children. The kid's menu has smaller servings and traditional favorites, offering a fun eating experience for the whole family.

Manufaktura Piwna, located on Piwna Street in the Old Town, is a welcoming restaurant for families with children. The menu offers a variety of Polish and European foods, and the rustic design provides a beautiful atmosphere. Children may play in a special play area, making it a great setting for families wanting to relax over a meal.

Bacówka is a great option for families looking to enjoy traditional Polish food. This restaurant, located in the Wrzeszcz neighborhood, serves regional delicacies like pierogi and substantial stews. The family-friendly atmosphere, along with excellent service, guarantees a genuine and memorable eating experience.

Bunkier Café, located near the historic Gdańsk Shipyard, is a fashionable family-friendly location. The menu combines Polish and foreign cuisine, and the contemporary design provides a lively ambiance. Bunkier Café often conducts family-friendly events, which provide additional entertainment for younger guests.

Pikawa, a family-friendly café in the Wrzeszcz neighborhood, serves wonderful pastries and sweets. Pikawa's pleasant environment and designated play space provide a calm atmosphere for families to enjoy coffee, pastries, and light meals. The kid-friendly menu guarantees that young children have a variety of delectable selections.

Pizza Hut in Gdańsk is a popular alternative for families looking for familiar and kid-friendly meals. Pizza Hut, located in the city center, provides a casual eating experience with a menu that includes pizzas, pasta dishes, and salads. The family-friendly setting and the ability to personalize meals make it a handy alternative for young customers.

Gdańsk's culinary environment welcomes families with a variety of kid-friendly establishments. From vegetarian delicacies to traditional Polish cuisines and worldwide favorites, these restaurants not only provide wonderful food but also create a pleasant setting for families to spend happy times around the dining table. Whether touring the Old Town or the open expanses of Oliwa, Gdańsk's kid-friendly eateries provide a fun and unforgettable family eating experience.

PARKS AND PLAYGROUNDS

Gdańsk is known for its historical beauty and marine attractions, but it also has parks and playgrounds that provide peaceful and enjoyable settings for families and guests. Gdańsk's parks provide a range of options, including peaceful retreats, scenic walks, and exciting playgrounds for children. Explore Gdańsk's green parks and fun places, making it an ideal location for outdoor aficionados.

Oliwa Park (Park Oliwski) is a lush green space in the Oliwa neighborhood that offers sculpted gardens, ponds, and walking routes. The park is known for its Oliwa Cathedral, but it also provides a peaceful setting for leisure and family picnics. Children may enjoy the attractive playgrounds spread around the park, guaranteeing a fun visit for the whole family.

Ronald Reagan Park (Park im. Ronalda Reagan), located in Gdańsk's Main Town, is a well-kept green area with groomed lawns, flowerbeds, and tree-lined walks. The park offers a serene getaway for those looking for a relaxing walk, and its central position makes it readily accessible. A playground inside the park provides a fun element, making it family-friendly.

Młody Grunwald (Young Grunwald) Park, located in the Wrzeszcz area, attracts both residents and tourists. The park has strolling trails, a pond, and plenty of foliage, providing a peaceful atmosphere. Families may enjoy picnics or let their children play on the well-equipped playgrounds, guaranteeing a fun excursion for all ages.

The Reagan Playground (Plac Zabaw i'm. Ronalda Reagan) is located near Ronald Reagan Park and offers a specialized place for children to explore and play. The playground is outfitted with contemporary structures, swings, and climbing frames, creating a safe and fun atmosphere for children. Its closeness to the park enables families to combine peaceful strolls with fun activities.

Dąbrowszczaków Park, located in the Orunia area, combines natural beauty with leisure activities. The park has strolling routes, a pond, and shaded areas, which contribute to its tranquil feel. A well-designed playground allows families to spend quality time in the beautiful surroundings.

Gdańsk Playground (Plac Zabaw Gdańsk) is located near the Gdańsk Shakespeare Theatre and offers a colorful environment for youngsters to play. Colorful play structures, slides, and swings appeal to a wide range of ages, making it an excellent choice for families touring the city center.

The Gdynia Playground (Plac Zabaw Gdynia) in the Wrzeszcz area offers a vibrant and well-maintained environment for youngsters. The playground has a variety of equipment, such as slides, climbing frames, and interactive components. Families may spend the day outside, surrounded by greenery and urban convenience.

Jasień Forest (Las Jasieński) provides a calm getaway on the outskirts of Gdańsk. The woodland has walking and bike pathways where families may immerse themselves in nature. Several clearings in the forest are ideal for picnics, providing a peaceful respite from the city.

The parks and playgrounds in Gdańsk strike a balance between nature and leisure. Whether you're touring historic districts or residential neighborhoods, these green oases and play places provide opportunities for relaxation, family connection, and delight in the bustling metropolitan. Gdańsk's outdoor areas, like the landmark Oliwa Park and the charming nooks of Ronald Reagan Park, encourage visitors to enjoy the beauty of nature and the endless energy of joyful discovery.

CHAPTER 15

GDAŃSK IN EVERY SEASON

SPRING IN GDAŃSK

Gdańsk evolves into a lovely refuge as the winter recedes and the first blooms sprout in the spring season. Spring in Gdańsk is a season of regeneration and brilliant hues, with flowering cherry trees in parks and colorful activities celebrating warmer days. Join us on a tour through the city's springtime appeal, when nature, culture, and the promise of better weather come together.

Spring revitalizes Gdańsk's parks and gardens with vibrant hues. Oliwa Park, with its majestic cathedral and groomed grounds, is filled with blooming cherry and magnolia trees. Ronald Reagan Park and Młody Grunwald Park have bloomed, providing a tranquil setting for walks and family trips.

Gdańsk celebrates spring with beautiful Cherry Blossom Festivals, particularly at Oliwa Park. These festivities are a visual feast, with the park's cherry trees bursting with beautiful pink and white blooms. Visitors may take part in cultural activities, picnics, and photography sessions among the magnificent cherry blossoms, creating a wonderfully magical atmosphere.

As temperatures increase, Gdańsk's outdoor cafés and riverbank eating spots come to life. The terraces along the Motława River in the Old Town and Sopot's pier provide ideal locations to enjoy a cup of coffee or a leisurely lunch while basking in the warm spring sun. The waterfront setting lends another element of appeal to dining encounters.

Springtime markets provide fresh fruit, unique goods, and brilliant flowers for both residents and tourists. The Long Market in Old Town and Hala Targowa are busy places to enjoy local delicacies, buy seasonal products, and experience the vibrant spirit of springtime trade.

Spring brings a vibrant cultural calendar in Gdańsk, with a variety of events and festivals. The city's cultural sector thrives in the spring, with art exhibits and music festivals. Consider attending performances at the Gdańsk Shakespeare Theatre or the European Solidarity Centre to enhance your spring stay with cultural flare.

Springtime on the Baltic Sea: With longer days and rising temperatures, the sea becomes a relaxing destination. Visit Sopot or Gdańsk beaches for a revitalizing coastal experience. While the water may still be cold, the seaside promenades and fresh sea air provide an ideal setting for lengthy walks and relaxing by the water.

Gdańsk celebrates Easter with vivid customs and festivities. The city's churches hold Easter services, and the Old Town comes alive with Easter marketplaces selling handcrafted goods, traditional meals, and colorful decorations. Join in the events to discover the region's rich cultural legacy.

Spring brings full bloom to Gdańsk's botanical and private gardens, in addition to parks. The Gdańsk University Botanical Garden offers a serene environment for nature lovers, with a wonderful collection of flowers and plants. Exploring private gardens in residential areas demonstrates the residents' inventiveness and love for creating their springtime retreats.

Spring in Gdańsk is a season of regeneration and celebration. The city's surroundings turn into a canvas of blossoming flowers and bright activities. Gdańsk celebrates spring with vibrant celebrations and stunning cherry blossoms in Oliwa Park. Springtime in Gdańsk invites you to appreciate the beauty and vigor of the changing season, whether you're sipping coffee on a balcony, attending cultural events, or wandering through the flowering parks.

SUMMER VIBES

As summer hits, Gdańsk transforms into a bustling city filled with vitality and sunlight. From the sun-kissed beaches along the Baltic Sea to the busy alleys of the Old Town, the city exudes a festive atmosphere that embodies the spirit of the season. Join us on a tour through the summer moods of Gdańsk, where outdoor activities, cultural celebrations, and coastline charm combine to create memorable memories.

Summer in Gdańsk welcomes beachgoers to the golden beaches of Sopot Beach. This famed Baltic Sea beach, located at a short distance from the city, is a sunbather's delight. Stretch out on a beach blanket, swim in the invigorating water, or wander down the bustling promenade packed with attractive cafés and bright beach clubs.

Gdańsk's seaside promenade exudes summer emotions. The Motława River, surrounded by old and contemporary structures, becomes a hive of activity. Take a stroll along the promenade, where street entertainers, outdoor cafés, and boat cruises provide a great blend of entertainment and relaxation.

Summer in Gdańsk has open-air concerts and events that bring the city to life with music. The city hosts a variety of musical genres, including classical concerts in the Gdańsk Shakespeare Theatre and contemporary music festivals in outdoor locations. Check the events calendar for live acts to bring some rhythm to your summer nights.

During the summer, Gdańsk's Old Town offers al fresco eating on its ancient streets. Choose from a variety of attractive cafés and eateries that flow out into the cobblestone squares. Enjoy traditional Polish foods, foreign cuisine, and cool drinks while taking in the atmosphere of this UNESCO-listed urban asset.

Summer Markets and Street Fairs: During the summer, Gdańsk's streets turn into colorful markets and street fairs, providing a variety of local crafts, artisanal items, and delectable food. Wander around the Long Market and Hala Targowa to soak up the vibrant ambiance, taste regional delicacies, and purchase one-of-a-kind gifts from local artists.

A cruise on the Motława River offers a unique view of Gdańsk. Many boat cruises provide panoramic views of the city's skyline, ancient shipyards, and famous monuments. Whether it's a midday sightseeing trip or a romantic night time sail, the river offers a picturesque background for unforgettable summer adventures.

Biking Adventures: Enjoy summer by exploring Gdańsk on two wheels. The city provides bike rentals, enabling you to peddle along designated cycling trails and explore the coastal regions. Ride through Oliwa Park, along the seashore boulevards, or explore the gorgeous suburbs for some fresh air and outdoor fun.

Westerplatte offers stunning sunset views over the Baltic Sea, perfect for a relaxing summer evening. This historic peninsula, famous for its involvement in World War II, offers a peaceful environment to reflect on the day and admire the changing hues of the sky as the sun sets on the horizon.

Summer in Gdańsk celebrates life, culture, and the city's beautiful beauty, drenched in sunlight. Gdańsk's summer moods provide a diverse range of activities, from lounging on the sandy beaches of Sopot to tasting local tastes in the Old Town and enjoying open-air performances along the waterfront. Immerse yourself in the warmth of the season, as every sun-kissed moment becomes a treasured memory in this bustling Polish metropolis.

AUTUMN COLORS

As summer passes and fall arrives, Gdańsk changes into a canvas painted with the rich colors of the season. Autumn in Gdańsk provides a unique visual and sensual experience, with golden leaves blanketing ancient streets and warm cafés in the Old Town. Join us on a tour of the city's fall hues, where nature, culture, and the changing seasons combine in a symphony of warmth and beauty.

Oliwa Park, noted for its lush foliage in spring and summer, transforms into a magnificent sight throughout fall. The park's stately trees, including oaks and maples, transform into bright tones of red, orange, and gold. Stroll around the park's meandering trails and see the reflection of autumn's splendor in the ponds that dot the gorgeous environment.

Historic Streets Gdańsk's Old Town, with its cobblestone streets and centuries-old buildings, transforms into a picturesque masterpiece throughout the autumn season. Autumn foliage's warm tones enhance the façade of colorful merchant buildings. Enjoy a leisurely stroll along Długa Street and Mariacka Street, where the contrast of old architecture and nature's fall palette creates a mesmerizing mood.

Ronald Reagan Park, a verdant oasis in the city center, provides a peaceful respite throughout the fall season. The park's trees, which include chestnuts and lindens, provide a stunning display of warm colors. Find a quiet seat, breathe in the cool air, and enjoy the calm of this autumn-themed urban sanctuary.

As temperatures drop, Gdańsk's Old Town cafés transform into cozy sanctuaries with autumnal aromas. Step inside these pleasant places, where the perfume of freshly brewed coffee blends with the smell of fall. Enjoy warm drinks, seasonal pastries, and watch the world go by from the coziness of a café, cocooned in the city's autumnal atmosphere.

Autumn brings a plethora of cultural events and festivals in Gdańsk. From cinema screenings to art exhibits, the city's venues come alive with cultural events. Fall programs at the European Solidarity Centre and Gdańsk Shakespeare Theatre provide a chance to enjoy the arts while surrounded by beautiful fall scenery.

Gdańsk's Autumn Markets and Harvest Bazaars provide a variety of seasonal products, including pumpkins, apples, and locally produced treats. Visit the Long Market and Hala Targowa to enjoy the fall harvest, sample regional delicacies, and bring home a taste of Gdańsk's seasonal tastes.

The Motława River, a key landmark of Gdańsk, reflects the changing hues of fall. Take a walk along the riverbank promenade, where ancient warehouses and waterfront cafés are accented with reflections of golden leaves floating down the river. Sunset walks by the canal provide a quiet and lovely view of fall in the city.

Nature areas around Gdańsk, like Sobieszewo Island and the Vistula Spit, provide stunning autumnal vistas to explore. Explore the walking paths, breathe in the fresh air, and watch migrating birds take flight against the background of golden foliage—the ideal escape for nature enthusiasts seeking the entire spectrum of October splendor.

Autumn in Gdańsk is a visual and sensual feast, transforming the metropolis into a masterpiece painted with warm seasonal colors. Gdańsk's Old Town and Oliwa Park provide a spectacular fall experience. Embrace the brisk air, indulge in the brightness of fall colors, and let the city's seasonal charm create lasting memories in this lovely Polish location.

WINTER MAGIC

Winter in Gdańsk turns the city into a magical paradise with dazzling lights and fresh air, creating a festive ambiance. Gdańsk offers a magical winter experience, with snug cafés and seasonal markets lining the streets. The city is rich in history and charm. Join us to discover what makes Gdańsk a fascinating winter destination.

Gdańsk's Old Town transforms into a stunning show of lights and decorations throughout the winter season. Historic structures, such as the landmark Main Town Hall and St. Mary's Basilica, are decked with glittering lights that give a pleasant glow over cobblestone streets. Take a leisurely walk around the lit Old Town to fully immerse yourself in the magical winter atmosphere.

Gdańsk's Main Town hosts Christmas markets, bringing festive excitement to the city. Wooden booths with decorations sell a range of holiday snacks, handicrafts, and ornaments. Indulge in traditional Polish specialties, drink mulled wine, and explore the market's enchanting ambiance, which is filled with the aroma of gingerbread and roasted chestnuts.

During the winter months, the Long Market has a temporary ice rink where visitors may enjoy ice skating beneath the open sky. The ice rink, surrounded by the ancient architecture of the Old Town, gives a touch of winter enchantment to this landmark area. Skating aficionados and families alike may enjoy this seasonal outdoor sport in the city's festive atmosphere.

The Gdańsk Shakespeare Theatre changes into a winter wonderland during colder months, holding events and plays. From theatrical shows to winter-themed activities, the theater offers a cultural vacation where visitors may enjoy the charm of the season inside its ancient walls.

Gdańsk offers cozy cafés and warm retreats to escape the cold winter weather. The Old Town is lined with restaurants that provide warm drinks, exquisite pastries, and a comfortable atmosphere. Step inside, relax by the fireplace and watch the metropolis outside change into a wintry scene.

St. Dominic's Fair in Winter: Continuing the tradition of the summer fair, the winter fair brings the same joyous energy. During the fair's winter version, the Main Town will offer extra markets, street performances, and cultural activities. Join in the fun, browse the booths, and bask in the festive ambiance that defines this holiday festival.

Gdańsk's parks and riverfront promenade look stunning when coated with snow. Winter hikes are ideal at Oliwa Park, Ronald Reagan Park, and along the Motława River. The cool air and calm mood make a peaceful getaway, enabling visitors to see the city's natural splendor in a new light.

Gdańsk offers lively New Year's Eve events to say goodbye to the previous year and welcome the new one. The Main Town Square is alive with celebrations, featuring live music, fireworks, and a celebratory mood. Join the city's residents and tourists as they count down to midnight in a joyous and exciting celebration.

Gdańsk is a winter wonderland that welcomes tourists to experience the charm of the season. From the colorful lights of the Old Town to the warmth of cafés and the joyful mood of Christmas markets, every aspect of the city exudes the spirit of winter. Gdańsk's winter offers a spectacular experience, whether you're gliding on an ice rink, discovering snow-covered parks, or participating in seasonal festivals.

CHAPTER 16

ITINERARIES FOR VARIOUS INTERESTS

HISTORY BUFF'S ITINERARY

Gdańsk's rich history and vital role in European heritage provide a thrilling experience for history aficionados. This tour explores Gdańsk's historical monuments, museums, and landmarks, providing insight into the city's cultural heritage.

Day 1: Old Town Time Travel

Morning:

- St. Mary's Church: Start your day by visiting St. Mary's Church, one of the world's biggest brick churches. Admire the Gothic architecture and climb the tower for panoramic views of Gdańsk.
- Explore the ancient Long Market (Długi Targ) with its colorful façade. Explore the Neptune Fountain, a symbol of Gdańsk's maritime heritage.

Afternoon:

- Artus Court: Visit Artus Court, a Renaissance-style edifice that previously functioned as a gathering place for merchants. Admire the architecture and explore the interior, which has an extensive collection of art and antiquities.

- The Golden Gate serves as an outstanding entry to the Royal Way, a historic thoroughfare through the center of Gdańsk.

Evening:

- meal in Old Town: For a typical Polish meal, visit one of Old Town's wonderful eateries. Consider Restauracja Kubicki or Piwna 47 Restaurant & Pub for a historical setting.

Day Two: Maritime Heritage and Solidarity.

Morning:

- Start your day visiting the National Maritime Museum on Granaries Island. Explore exhibitions about shipbuilding, naval history, and marine customs. Don't miss the magnificent shipyard cranes outside.
- Gdańsk Shipyards: Visit the historic cradle of the Solidarity movement. Visit the Monument to the Fallen Shipyard Workers and consider the city's role in the struggle for workers' rights.

Afternoon:

- European Solidarity Centre: Learn about the history of

the Solidarity movement at the European Solidarity Center. Interactive exhibits, multimedia displays, and testimonies provide a complete picture of this critical period.

- Solidarity Square: Spend time in Solidarity Square, where significant events in the Solidarity movement occurred. The Monument to the Fallen Shipyard Workers may be found in this significant place.

Evening:

- Dinner at the Shipyard District: Immerse yourself in the historic environment while dining. Consider Pierogarnia u Dzika for great pierogi or Pivarium, which serves artisan beer in a shipyard environment.

Day 3: we explore Oliwa and its cultural heritage.

Morning:

- Travel to the Oliwa neighborhood to see the Oliwa Cathedral. Admire the Baroque architecture and attend an organ performance to hear the cathedral's acoustics.
- Oliwa Park: Enjoy a stroll around Oliwa Park, a peaceful green environment with ponds, bridges, and walking routes.

Afternoon:

- Oliwa Zoo: Those interested in nature and animals should pay a visit to Oliwa Zoo, which is situated close to the cathedral and park.
- Lunch in Oliwa: For a delicious lunch, visit a local restaurant in Oliwa. Cafe Ferber and Kawiarnia Oliwia are great choices.

Evening:

- Return to Old Town to spend the evening at Literacka Café. Enjoy the bohemian atmosphere, maybe with a book or in a chat with the locals.
- This itinerary delves into Gdańsk's history, including medieval architecture and

major events that affected the city in the 20th century. Explore Gdańsk's rich cultural and marine heritage and see its interesting history.

ART AND CULTURE ENTHUSIAST'S GUIDE

Gdańsk, a city rich in history, art, and maritime heritage, is a must-see for art and culture enthusiasts. This book takes you on a tour of museums, galleries, and cultural sites, providing insight into the heart of this charming Baltic city.

Day 1: Old Town Treasures

Morning:

- The Gdansk Museum of Art (Muzeum Narodowe w Gdańsku): Begin your cultural excursion in the Gdańsk Museum of Art, situated in the center of Old Town. Admire a broad selection of Polish and European art from different times.
- Wander around Mariacka Street, which is famed for its handcrafted amber stores and historical charm. Discover the delicate detailing on the Renaissance-style façade.

Afternoon:

- The National Museum in Gdańsk's Main Building (Muzeum Narodowe -

Główne) offers a comprehensive exploration of Polish art history. The museum has a stunning collection of paintings, sculptures, and decorative arts.

- For lunch in Old Town, visit a pleasant café or restaurant like Cafe Ferber or Gdańska Restaurant to enjoy a meal while admiring the old architecture.

Evening:

- Explore the Amber Museum (Muzeum Bursztynu), located in a medieval jail complex. Discover the history of amber in Gdańsk, including its importance in art and handicraft.

- Dinner at Restauracja Kubicki: Finish your day with a delicious meal at Restauracja Kubicki, a restaurant with a long history and an artistic atmosphere.

Day 2 - Maritime Heritage and Contemporary Art

Morning:

- Return to the National Maritime Museum and see the exhibits on Granaries Island. Explore marine art, ship models, and nautical artifacts.
- Gdansk Crane (Żuraw): Visit Gdańsk Crane, a famous

waterfront landmark. Discover its origins as a medieval port crane and its importance in the city's maritime trade.

Afternoon:

- Explore the Gdańsk Shipyard Walls, where colorful murals and public art commemorate the city's shipbuilding history. The region has become a canvas for both local and international artists.
- Lunch at Pivarium: Enjoy a relaxed lunch at Pivarium, a craft beer tavern in the Shipyard District famed for its industrial-chic vibe.

Evening:

- Explore contemporary art galleries in Gdańsk, including the Laznia Centre for Contemporary Art and the Gdańsk City Gallery. Immerse yourself in the city's vibrant art scene.
- Finish the day with supper at Brovarnia Gdańsk, a brewery and restaurant located in a historic granary structure.

Day three: Oliwa's elegance and bohemian vibes

Morning:

- Oliwa Cathedral and Park: Visit Oliwa Cathedral. Admire the Baroque interiors and hear an organ performance. Take a leisurely walk around Oliwa Park, a beautiful green paradise.

Afternoon:

- Visit Wyspa Słodowa (Malt Island), a creative location recognized for its bohemian vibe and street art. The island holds cultural events and meetings, offering a unique view of Gdańsk's alternative culture.
- Lunch at Kawiarnia Oliwia: Enjoy lunch at Kawiarnia Oliwia, a beautiful café in Oliwa noted for its welcoming environment and delicious handmade cuisine.

Evening:

- Literacka Café: Return to Old Town and spend the evening at Literacka Café. Immerse yourself in the bohemian atmosphere, complete with literature and local art. Engage in discussion with other customers or just enjoy the artsy atmosphere.
- This guide for art and culture enthusiasts explores Gdańsk's rich creative heritage. From medieval masterpieces to modern expressions, the city's cultural riches will make an indelible impact on every art and culture enthusiast.

FOODIE'S DELIGHT

Gdańsk's culinary legacy and dynamic food scene make it a must-visit destination for foodies. From traditional Polish meals to foreign tastes, this guide will take you on a culinary tour through the city's greatest restaurants and local delicacies.

Day 1 - Polish Culinary Classics

Morning:

- Breakfast at Pierogarnia Mandu: Begin your day at Pierogarnia Mandu, a quaint restaurant that serves a variety of pierogi (dumplings) with traditional and unique fillings. Pair them with a cup of fragrant Polish coffee.

Afternoon:

- For lunch, visit Gdańska Restaurant located in the center of Old Town. Experience traditional Polish meals like Bigos (hunter's stew), Golonka (pork knuckle), and Żurek (sour rye soup) in a historical atmosphere.

Evenings:

- Dinner at Goldwasser: For a more expensive dining experience, visit Goldwasser, which is noted for its exquisite environment and Polish delicacies. Try the popular regional dish, Klopsiki po Gdańsku (Gdańsk-style meatballs).

Day Two: Seafood Extravaganza
Morning:

- Visit Gdynia Fish Market: Take a quick trip to Gdynia Fish Market to enjoy the lively atmosphere and buy fresh seafood. Take a leisurely walk and appreciate the seashore scenery.

Afternoon:

- Return to Gdańsk and have lunch at Zielona Weranda. Enjoy a seafood feast with Baltic herring, smoked salmon, and other local favorites cooked with a contemporary twist.

Evening:

- Enjoy a seaside supper at Restauracja Molo, situated on the Motława River. Enjoy grilled fish and seafood platters with magnificent views of Gdańsk's historic waterfront.

Day three: Sweet indulgences and local treats.

Morning:

- Gdańska Manufaktura Czekolady serves coffee and pastries. Start your day with a visit to Gdańska

Manufaktura Czekolady, where you can enjoy great coffee, chocolates, and pastries.

Afternoon:

- Enjoy a substantial lunch at Stągiewna, a restaurant that specializes in regional food. Try meals such as Pstrąg Po Kaszubsku (Kashubian-style fish) and Kartacz (potato dumplings).

Evening:

- Finish your gastronomic adventure at Taverna Dominikańska, a medieval tavern in Old Town. In a lovely medieval environment, you may enjoy traditional Polish foods.

Additional foodie experiences:

Street Food Exploration:

- Wander through the alleyways of Old Town to find street food carts selling local goodies like Oscypek (smoked sheep cheese) and Zapiekanka (a Polish open-faced sandwich).

Craft Beer Tasting:

- Visit craft beer establishments like Brovarnia Gdańsk or Pivarium to try local and regional craft beers, along with traditional Polish delicacies.

Visit the Milk Bar (Bar Mleczny):

- Experience the nostalgia of a typical Milk Bar, such as Bar Mleczny Neptun, for inexpensive and genuine Polish comfort food.

Try sweets at Lodziarnia:

- Lodziarnia serves handcrafted ice cream and pastries, including the popular Pączki (Polish doughnuts).

Gdańsk's culinary scene offers a diverse range of tastes that combine Baltic and Polish traditions. Whether you're eating pierogi, enjoying fresh seafood on the waterfront, or visiting local markets, the city is a foodie's paradise that embraces the diversity of Polish cuisine.

ADVENTURE SEEKER'S ROUTE

This route in Gdańsk offers outdoor sports, marine exploration, and off-the-beaten-path excursions for those seeking excitement during their vacation. Prepare to go on an adventure that mixes thrilling encounters with the distinctive charm of this ancient city.

Day 1: Waterfront Adventures

Morning:

- Start your journey by kayaking on the Motława River. Paddle through the historic center of Gdańsk, past notable monuments like the Gdańsk Crane and the Green Gate.

Afternoon:

- Jet Skiing in the Baltic Sea: Visit the Baltic Sea for an adrenaline-fueled jet skiing's adventure. Experience the thrill of the sea wind as you race over the waves, taking in panoramic views of the Gdańsk coastline.

Evening:

- Stągiewna, a maritime-themed restaurant, offers a delicious supper to replenish your energy. Enjoy seafood delights and a laid-back environment in the heart of Old Town.

Day 2: Urban Exploration, High Ropes

Morning:

- Urban High Ropes at Kolibki Adventure Park: Test your skills with a morning session of urban high ropes at Kolibki Adventure Park. Navigate through treetop obstacles and zip lines for an exhilarating start to the day.

Afternoon:

- Lunch at So Hanami: Refuel with a fast lunch at So Hanami, which serves a blend of Asian tastes. The vivid and sophisticated surroundings create a striking contrast to the morning's outdoor trip.

Evening:

- Explore Abandoned Shipyard regions: For a unique experience, visit the abandoned shipyard regions. Explore Gdańsk's industrial heritage via graffiti-covered buildings and a raw urban vibe.

Day three: Sand dunes and quad biking.

Morning:

- Visit Sobieszewo Island Beach for an unforgettable beach experience. Explore Ptasi Raj's white sand dunes and enjoy the nature reserve's pristine splendor.

Afternoon:

- Quad bike experience: Venture to the fringes for an exhilarating quad bike experience. Navigate through woodland paths and vast fields while enjoying the excitement of off-road quad riding.

Evening:

- beachfront campfire: Round up your adventure-filled day with a beachfront campfire on Sobieszewo Island. Relax, tell tales, and enjoy the tranquil atmosphere of the Baltic Sea beneath the twilight sky.

Additional adventure experiences:

Parasailing in Sopot.

- Experience the thrill of parasailing over Gdańsk Bay with a short excursion to Sopot, offering breathtaking aerial views.

Sandboarding at Sobieszewo:

- Sandboarding on the dunes of Sobieszewo Island combines the exhilaration of surfing with the distinctive Baltic coast environment.

Escape Room Experience:

- Escape rooms in Gdańsk provide a team-based challenge to solve riddles and reveal secrets.

Bungee jump in Gdynia:

- For the ultimate adrenaline thrill, try bungee jumping in neighboring Gdynia, which overlooks the Baltic Sea.

Gdańsk offers adventurers a variety of experiences, including nautical activities, urban difficulties, and natural beauties. This route offers an unparalleled combination of excitement, discovery, and the fascinating beauty of this Baltic city.

CHAPTER 17

LANGUAGE AND TRAVEL PHRASEBOOK

ESSENTIAL PHRASES AND EXPRESSIONS

While English is widely spoken in tourist areas, knowing a few basic Polish phrases can greatly enhance your travel experience in Gdańsk. The locals appreciate the effort, and it can contribute to a more immersive and enjoyable stay. Here are some essential phrases and expressions to help you navigate daily interactions in Gdańsk:

1. Greetings:

- Dzień dobry: Good morning / Good afternoon
- Dobry wieczór: Good evening
- Dobranoc: Good night

2. Basic Politeness:

- Proszę: Please
- Dziękuję: Thank you
- Przepraszam: Excuse me / I'm sorry
- Proszę bardzo: You're welcome

3. Common Courtesies:

- Tak: Yes
- Nie: No
- Proszę nie: Please don't
- Przepraszam, nie rozumiem: I'm sorry, I don't understand

4. Introductions:

- Jak się masz? / Jak się pan/pani ma?: How are you? (informal/formal)
- Nazywam się [your name]: My name is [your name]
- Miło mi: Nice to meet you

5. Directions and Navigation:

- Gdzie jest...?: Where is...?
- Prawo/lewo: Right/left
- Prosto: Straight ahead
- Czy mogę prosić o pomoc?: Can I ask for help?

6. Ordering Food and Drinks:

- Menu, proszę: The menu, please

- Chciałbym/Chciałabym...: I would like... (male/female)
- Jestem wegetarianinem/wegetariank ą: I am a vegetarian (male/female)
- Rachunek, proszę: The bill, please

7. Numbers:

- Jeden: One
- Dwa: Two
- Trzy: Three
- Dziesięć: Ten
- Sto: One hundred

8. Time and Dates:

- Która jest godzina?: What time is it?
- Dziś: Today
- Jutro: Tomorrow

- Wczoraj: Yesterday

9. Shopping Phrases:

- Ile to kosztuje?: How much does it cost?
- Czy można dostać paragon?: Can I have a receipt?
- Czy akceptujecie kartę kredytową?: Do you accept credit cards?

10. Emergency Phrases:

- Pomocy!: Help!
- Jestem zagubiony/zagubiona: I am lost (male/female)
- Proszę wezwać pomoc: Please call for help

11. Miscellaneous:

- Gdzie jest toaleta?: Where is the bathroom?
- Czy mówisz po angielsku?: Do you speak English?
- Nie rozumiem po polsku: I don't understand Polish

Remember, the effort to speak a few local phrases is appreciated, and many Poles will gladly switch to English if they see you're trying. Don't be afraid to ask for clarification or repetition, and enjoy the cultural exchange as you explore the charming streets of Gdańsk.

LANGUAGE TIPS FOR TRAVELERS

While English is widely spoken in tourist areas, incorporating a few Polish phrases and understanding certain language nuances can enhance your communication and cultural experience in Gdańsk. Here are some language tips to help you navigate conversations and make the most of your time in this charming Baltic city:

1. Learn Basic Polish Phrases: Familiarize yourself with essential phrases such as greetings, thank you, and common courtesies. This effort demonstrates respect for the local language and culture.
Basic phrases like "Dzień dobry" (Good morning/afternoon),

"Proszę" (Please), and "Dziękuję" (Thank you) go a long way.

2. Use Politeness Titles: When addressing someone formally, use "Pan" (Mr.) for men and "Pani" (Mrs./Ms.) for women followed by their surname. This shows respect, especially in more formal situations.

3. Practice Pronunciation: Polish pronunciation can be challenging for non-native speakers. Practice common phrases and place names to feel more confident when speaking. Pay attention to letter combinations like "cz," "sz," and "rz."

4. Use Numbers: Familiarize yourself with basic numbers, especially when dealing with

prices, quantities, or addresses. This can be particularly useful when shopping, ordering food, or using public transportation.

5. Understand Formality: Polish has formal and informal ways of addressing people. Use the formal "Pan" and "Pani" when addressing strangers, older individuals, or in more professional settings. The informal "ty" is used among friends and peers.

6. Be Patient and Ask for Clarification: If you encounter difficulties in understanding or expressing yourself, don't hesitate to ask for clarification. Poles appreciate the effort, and many will gladly assist you or switch to English if necessary.

7. Take Advantage of Language Apps: Utilize language learning apps that offer Polish lessons. Apps like Duolingo, Babbel, or Memrise can provide basic language skills and pronunciation practice.

8. Use English Pronunciations for Some Words: Some Polish words are commonly used in English with an anglicized pronunciation. For example, "Gdańsk" is often pronounced as "Gdansk" in English.

9. Engage Locals with Respect: Poles appreciate when visitors attempt to speak their language. However, if someone responds to you in English, don't insist on continuing in Polish if they seem more comfortable in English.

10. Learn About Local Customs: Understanding cultural nuances can help you communicate more effectively. For example, addressing people by their first name may be considered informal, and handshakes are a common greeting.

11. Consider a Phrasebook: Carry a small phrasebook that includes common phrases and expressions. This can be a quick reference guide for situations where language assistance is needed.

12. Attend Language Exchange Events: Look for language exchange events or meetups where you can practice Polish with locals or other travelers. This can be a fun and interactive way to improve your language skills.

By embracing the local language and showing a willingness to communicate in Polish, you can create more meaningful connections and gain a deeper appreciation for the rich cultural tapestry of Gdańsk. The locals will likely appreciate your efforts, and you may find yourself immersed in a more authentic travel experience.

CHAPTER 18

APPENDIX

MAPS OF GDAŃSK

Exploring the enchanting city of Gdańsk is made more accessible and enjoyable with the assistance of maps. From historic landmarks to hidden gems, having the right maps ensures that you can navigate the city efficiently and make the most of your visit. Whether you prefer traditional paper maps or digital navigation tools, Gdańsk provides a wealth of resources to help you discover its rich history, vibrant culture, and picturesque landscapes.

1. Paper Maps:

- Tourist Information Centers: Gdańsk is equipped with tourist information centers scattered across key locations, including the airport, train station, and the Old Town. These centers provide free city maps with detailed information about attractions, public transport, and useful tips.
- City Guides and Brochures: Many hotels, museums, and popular attractions offer informative brochures and city guides that often include detailed maps. These resources are handy for on-the-go reference and usually provide

additional insights into Gdańsk's attractions.

2. Online Maps:

- Google Maps: The ubiquitous Google Maps is a reliable tool for navigating Gdańsk. It offers detailed maps of streets, landmarks, and public transport routes. You can use it both on desktop and as a mobile app for real-time navigation.
- VisitGdańsk Website: The official tourism website for Gdańsk often provides downloadable maps that you can print or use digitally. These maps may include suggested walking routes, key attractions, and transportation information.

- Citymapper: If you're relying on public transport, Citymapper is a user-friendly app that provides real-time information about buses, trams, and other modes of transportation in Gdańsk. It also suggests the best routes for walking or cycling.

3. Specialized Maps:

- Historical Maps: For those interested in Gdańsk's rich history, some specialized maps focus on historical sites, allowing you to trace the city's evolution through different periods. These maps are available in certain museums or can be found in historical literature.

- Culinary and Shopping Maps: Some maps cater specifically to food enthusiasts or shoppers, guiding you to the best culinary spots or the most exciting shopping districts in Gdańsk. Check with local tourism offices for these specialized maps.

4. Mobile Apps:

- Gdańsk Official App: Many cities, including Gdańsk, have their own official apps that offer maps, event schedules, and practical information for tourists. Check if Gdańsk has an official app to enhance your exploration experience.

- Offline Maps Apps: Consider downloading offline maps for Gdańsk through apps like MAPS.ME or Here WeGo. This ensures you have access to maps even when you're without an internet connection, particularly useful for international travelers.

5. Navigation Signage:

- Street Signs: Gdańsk has well-marked streets with clear signage, making it easy to navigate on foot or by car. Street signs are typically in Polish, but many important ones also include English translations.

- Tourist Signage: Look out for tourist-oriented signs pointing towards major attractions, landmarks, and historical sites. These signs are strategically placed to guide visitors through the city's highlights.

Equipping yourself with the right maps and navigation tools ensures a seamless and enriching experience in Gdańsk. Whether you prefer the tactile feel of a paper map or the convenience of digital navigation, the city offers a variety of resources to help you explore its captivating streets, historic sites, and vibrant neighborhoods. As you embark on your Gdańsk adventure, let the maps be your reliable companions, guiding you through the cultural treasures and hidden gems of this maritime jewel on the Baltic coast.

USEFUL CONTACTS

When exploring Gdańsk, it's beneficial to have a list of essential contacts to ensure a smooth and enjoyable experience. Whether you need assistance with travel arrangements, require information about local services, or in case of emergencies, these contacts will prove invaluable during your stay. Here's a comprehensive list of useful contacts in Gdańsk:

1. Emergency Services:

    - Emergency (Police, Fire, Ambulance): 112

- Police (Local): 997
- Fire Department (Local): 998
- Ambulance (Local): 999

2. Medical Assistance:

- Emergency Medical Services: 999
- Gdańsk Emergency Hospital (Szpital Miejski im. J. Strusia): +48 58 768 06 00
- Pharmacies: Look for the green cross sign; 24-hour pharmacies are available, and their locations can be found online or by asking locals.

3. Tourist Information:

- Gdańsk Tourist Information Center: +48 58 301 43 55

- Address: Długi Targ 28/29, 80-830 Gdańsk, Poland
- Email: informacja@visitgdansk.com
- Gdańsk Lech Wałęsa Airport Tourist Information: +48 58 348 11 11

4. Transportation:

- Gdańsk Lech Wałęsa Airport: +48 58 348 11 11
- Gdańsk Główny (Main Railway Station): +48 703 200 200
- Public Transport Information (ZTM Gdańsk): +48 58 721 77 77

5. Embassies and Consulates:

- U.S. Consulate General in Gdańsk: +48 22 504 2000
- Emergency: +48 601 483 348
- British Honorary Consulate in Gdańsk: +48 58 772 09 59
- Emergency: +48 602 450 645
- Canadian Honorary Consulate in Gdańsk: +48 58 349 09 95
- Emergency: +48 602 232 195

6. City Services:

- Municipal Office (Urząd Miejski): +48 58 526 40 00
- Gdańsk Police Headquarters: +48 58 721 72 00

- City Guard (Straż Miejska): +48 58 322 20 00

7. Consular Assistance (for non-EU tourists):

- Gdańsk Foreigners' Office (Wydział Spraw Cudzoziemców): +48 58 323 60 00

8. Airport Information:

- Gdańsk Lech Wałęsa Airport Information: +48 58 348 11 11
- Lost and Found: +48 58 348 12 60

9. Public Services:

- Emergency Roadside Assistance (Pomoc Drogowa): 981
- Weather Forecast: Check reliable weather websites or apps for up-to-date information.

10. Language Assistance:

- Translator Services: If needed, contact your embassy or consulate for assistance.

11. Local Media:

- Trojmiasto.pl (Local News Website): www.trojmiasto.pl
- Radio Gdańsk (Local Radio Station): +48 58 322 88 10

- Gdańsk TV (Local Television): www.gdansk.pl/tv

12. Utilities and Services:

- Emergency Gas Service: 992
- Emergency Electricity Service: 991
- Emergency Water Service: 993

Remember to save these contacts in your phone or keep them in a readily accessible location during your visit to Gdańsk. Having these numbers at your fingertips ensures that you can quickly seek assistance, information, or necessary services, allowing you to focus on enjoying your time in this captivating Baltic city.

EMERGENCY INFORMATION

When traveling to Gdańsk, it's crucial to be familiar with emergency information to ensure your safety and well-being. Whether you encounter a medical issue, require police assistance, or face other emergency situations, knowing the appropriate contacts and procedures is essential. Here's a comprehensive guide to emergency information in Gdańsk:

1. General Emergency Contacts:

    - Emergency (Police, Fire, Ambulance): 112
    - Police (Local): 997
    - Fire Department (Local): 998
    - Ambulance (Local): 999

2. Medical Emergencies:

- Emergency Medical Services: Dial 999 for immediate medical assistance.
- Gdańsk Emergency Hospital (Szpital Miejski im. J. Strusia): +48 58 768 06 00
- Pharmacies: Look for the green cross sign; 24-hour pharmacies are available.

3. Tourist Assistance:

- Gdańsk Tourist Information Center: +48 58 301 43 55
- Address: Długi Targ 28/29, 80-830 Gdańsk, Poland
- Email: informacja@visitgdansk.com

- Gdańsk Lech Wałęsa Airport Tourist Information: +48 58 348 11 11

4. Transportation Emergencies:

- Gdańsk Lech Wałęsa Airport: +48 58 348 11 11
- Gdańsk Główny (Main Railway Station): +48 703 200 200
- Public Transport Information (ZTM Gdańsk): +48 58 721 77 77

5. Embassies and Consulates:

- U.S. Consulate General in Gdańsk: +48 22 504 2000
- Emergency: +48 601 483 348

- British Honorary Consulate in Gdańsk: +48 58 772 09 59
- Emergency: +48 602 450 645
- Canadian Honorary Consulate in Gdańsk: +48 58 349 09 95
- Emergency: +48 602 232 195

6. City Services:

- Municipal Office (Urząd Miejski): +48 58 526 40 00
- Gdańsk Police Headquarters: +48 58 721 72 00
- City Guard (Straż Miejska): +48 58 322 20 00

7. Consular Assistance (for non-EU tourists):

- Gdańsk Foreigners' Office (Wydział Spraw Cudzoziemców): +48 58 323 60 00

8. Airport Information:

- Gdańsk Lech Wałęsa Airport Information: +48 58 348 11 11
- Lost and Found: +48 58 348 12 60

9. Utilities and Services:

- Emergency Roadside Assistance (Pomoc Drogowa): 981
- Emergency Gas Service: 992
- Emergency Electricity Service: 991

- Emergency Water Service: 993

10. Language Assistance:

- Translator Services: If needed, contact your embassy or consulate for assistance.

Remember:

When dialing emergency numbers, operators often speak Polish, so having basic Polish phrases can be helpful.
Carry your identification, insurance information, and contact details for your country's embassy or consulate.
Familiarize yourself with the location of the nearest hospitals,

pharmacies, and emergency services in your vicinity.

By being aware of these emergency contacts and taking necessary precautions, you can enjoy your time in Gdańsk with confidence, knowing that assistance is readily available in case of any unforeseen circumstances.

CHAPTER 19

INDEX

QUICK REFERENCE FOR KEY TOPICS

1. Overview of Gdańsk:

- Location: Northern Poland, on the Baltic Sea
- Historical Significance: Hanseatic port, maritime trade hub
- Architectural Highlights: Old Town, Gothic and Renaissance buildings
- Cultural Charm: Maritime museums, vibrant festivals

2. Brief History:

- Founded: 10th century
- Hanseatic Era: Prosperous trading city
- WWII and Solidarity Movement: Significance in modern history
- Post-communist Era: Economic growth and cultural revival

3. Why Visit Gdańsk in 2024:

- Rich History: Explore medieval Old Town and historic shipyards
- Maritime Heritage: Visit maritime museums and sail on the Motława River
- Cultural Events: Attend festivals, concerts, and art exhibitions

- Solidarity Square: Experience the birthplace of the Solidarity movement

4. Best Time to Visit Gdańsk:

- Summer (June to August): Warm weather, vibrant festivals
- Spring (April to May) and Fall (September to October): Mild temperatures, fewer crowds
- Winter (December to February): Festive atmosphere, Christmas markets

5. Visa Requirements:

- EU, EEA, and Swiss citizens: No visa required

- Non-EU citizens: Check visa requirements based on nationality
- Schengen Zone: Poland is part of the Schengen Agreement

6, Currency and Budgeting Tips:

- Currency: Polish złoty (PLN)
- Budget: Moderate, with affordable dining options
- Tipping: 10-15% in restaurants, rounding up in cafes

7. Transportation Options:

- Lech Wałęsa Airport: International flights
- Public Transport: Trams, buses, and water trams

- Walking: Explore Old Town on foot
- Taxi and Ride-Sharing: Readily available

8. City Layout and Neighborhoods:

- Old Town: Historic center with medieval architecture
- Stare Miasto (Main Town): Central area with shops and restaurants
- Oliwa: Tranquil district with a cathedral and park
- Shipyard District: Historic site of Solidarity movement

9. Local Culture and Customs:

- Hospitality: Poles are welcoming and appreciate polite gestures

- Traditional Cuisine: Pierogi, kiełbasa, and Żurek are local specialties
- Festivals: Participate in cultural events and celebrations
- Respect for History: Sensitivity to WWII and Solidarity history

10. Language Essentials:

- Polish is the official language
- English is widely spoken in tourist areas
- Basic Polish phrases appreciated

11. The Royal Way:

- Historical Route: Walk from the Golden Gate to the Green Gate
- Landmarks: Neptune Fountain, Artus Court, and Long Market
- Rich Architecture: Gothic, Renaissance, and Baroque buildings

12. Old Town Highlights:

- Uplifting Architecture: St. Mary's Church, Town Hall, and Crane
- Market Square: Center of activities with shops and cafes
- Amber District: Explore the Amber Museum and boutiques

13. Solidarity Square and Monument:

- Historical Significance: Birthplace of Solidarity movement
- Monument to the Fallen Shipyard Workers: Iconic memorial
- European Solidarity Centre: Museum documenting Solidarity's history

14. Gdańsk Shipyards:

- Historical Significance: Birthplace of the Solidarity movement
- Monument to the Fallen Shipyard Workers: Iconic memorial

- European Solidarity Centre: Museum documenting Solidarity's history

15. Oliwa Cathedral and Park:

- Architectural Gem: Baroque cathedral with ornate interiors
- Oliwa Park: Tranquil park with walking paths and a pond
- Oliwa Zoo: Nearby attraction for nature enthusiasts

16. National Maritime Museum:

- Maritime Heritage: Exhibits on shipbuilding and naval history

- Granaries Island: Location of the museum with scenic views
- Shipyard Cranes: Iconic symbols of Gdańsk's maritime history

17. St. Mary's Church Museum:

- Gothic Marvel: St. Mary's Church, one of the world's largest brick churches
- Astronomical Clock: Historic clock with intricate mechanisms
- Tower Climb: Panoramic views of Gdańsk from the church tower

18. European Solidarity Centre:

- Interactive Museum: Chronicles the history of Solidarity movement
- Exhibits: Multimedia displays, artifacts, and interviews
- Memorial Wall: Commemorates those involved in the Solidarity movement

19. Artus Court:

- Renaissance Beauty: Historical building in the heart of Old Town
- Main Hall: Lavishly decorated space for banquets and events
- Amber Cabinets: Exhibit of precious amber artifacts

20. Amber Museum:

- Baltic Gold: Showcases the history and cultural significance of amber
- Amber Room Reproduction: Replica of the legendary Amber Room
- Interactive Exhibits: Hands-on activities and workshops

21. Traditional Polish Cuisine:

- Pierogi: Dumplings with various fillings
- Żurek: Hearty sour rye soup
- Bigos: Hunter's stew with sauerkraut and meats
- Kotlet Schabowy: Breaded and fried pork cutlet
- Gołąbki: Stuffed cabbage rolls

22. Gdańsk's Local Specialties:

- Łosoś z Platera: Platter of smoked salmon
- Ryba po Kaszubsku: Kashubian-style fish
- Smażony Śledź: Fried herring
- Gdańska Marynarka: Gdańsk Navy Rum
- Ciasto Francuskie: French pastry

23. Popular Restaurants and Cafés:

- Restauracja Kubicki: Elegant dining with a traditional Polish menu
- Piwna 47 Restaurant & Pub: Cozy pub atmosphere with Polish and European dishes
- Grand Cru Restaurant: Upscale dining with a focus

on modern European cuisine
- Literacka Café: Bohemian café with literary ambiance
- Gdańska Manufaktura Czekolady: Chocolate shop and café offering artisanal treats

24. Street Food Scene:

- Zapiekanka Stalls: Open-faced baguettes with various toppings
- Obwarzanki Stands: Ring-shaped bread snacks with seeds or salt
- Fish Snacks: Grilled or smoked fish on a stick
- Grilled Kielbasa Stands: Grilled Polish sausages
- Pączki: Polish doughnuts with assorted fillings

This quick reference guide provides a comprehensive overview of key topics in Gdańsk, offering a convenient resource for travelers seeking information on the city's history, attractions, cuisine, and practical tips for an enriching experience in this captivating maritime destination.

Printed in Great Britain
by Amazon

45173846R00215